Radical Feminists of

HETERODOXY

Greenwich Village 1912-1940

D1599071

by Judith Schwarz

CARL A. RUDISILL LIBRARY
LENOIR-RHYNE COLLEGE

WITHDRAWN

Revised edition
Copyright 1986, New Victoria Publishers, Inc.

No part of this book may be reproduced in any form without the permission
of the publisher.

All photographs (except where otherwise indicated) are from "Heterodoxy
to Marie" album, Inez Haynes Irwin Papers, and are reproduced with the
permission of The Schlesinger Library, Radcliffe College, Cambridge,
Massachusetts. We thank them for their interest and support.

Edited by Claudia Lamperti and Beth Dingman

Ha
1906
.N5
S38
1986
14 884 2
may 1990

Library of Congress # 86-062342
ISBN 0-934678-08-1

NEW VICTORIA PUBLISHERS, INC.

Box 27 Norwich, Vermont 05055

Table of Contents

List of Illustrations

Title Page of "Heterodoxy To Marie" Club Album

Preface

Ever since 1976, when I first saw the "Heterodoxy to Marie" photograph album given to club founder Marie Jenney Howe in 1920, I have been fascinated with Heterodoxy.[1] As I leafed through the black-and-white images of over sixty women, stopping along the way to read poems and inscriptions beneath many of the photographs, it was clear that this album glowed with love, respect and warm admiration. It was not only the members' obvious delight in Marie Howe that came through, but an almost over-whelming sense from each woman of real kinship with the other Heterodoxy members. Together, they knew that they had created something unique. They valued the experience of Heterodoxy meetings as much as they valued and enjoyed each other.

My surprise wasn't that a group of women should feel this way about other women—not at all. It wasn't that simple. My feelings came from the images themselves. Some of the women were quite matronly and maternal-looking, some of them fashionably avant-garde in the style of the time, and others were strikingly beautiful in a classic, timeless sense. Still, a large number of the women were also astonishingly tailored. Or, as my mind instantly reacted: "How butchy looking!" Using little or no make-up or jewelry, these women wore ties, high stiff collars, mannish suits and hats and simple short hair styles. They looked unflinchingly into the camera, full-face, with just a trace of a smile around the corners of their mouths. They looked like women with a secret they dared the viewer to discover. These particular women preferred to be presented in the album in informal snapshots, taken on a city street or during a country picnic.

I was also surprised by the obvious differences in the members' ages. The youngest looked in their twenties, while the oldest women were certainly around fifty, including Marie Howe. My knowledge, both personal and book-learned, of women's organizations in present-day America did not lead me to expect that a cohesive women's group would enjoy that wide an age range, nor such a difference in lives as reflected in the outward clothing and appearances of the members. It did not surprise me that the club members appeared to be an all-white group, although I was pleasantly surprised that a group existing in New York in 1912 included many Jewish and Irish members. (One would be hard put to find a men's organization of that era with a similarly broad range of membership.) Later, I learned that member Grace Nail Johnson was a prominent light-skinned Black woman, active in Harlem social and literary circles as well as in the National Association for the Advancement of Colored People (NAACP). She was the only Black member thus far found, although several Black women attended meetings as guests. Once again, my own limited experience in groups and knowledge of the ethnic prejudices of Heterodoxy's time period led me to expect less diversity in racial, cultural and religious background. (This was, of course, before I learned more about the women of Heterodoxy, and how much they varied in so many ways from the expected.) Even by the

1960s and 70s, few of the feminist and lesbian groups I belonged to had more than a few Black, Hispanic, Chicana or Asian women members. Looking through Heterodoxy's photographs, I began to realize that with few exceptions, the women's groups I knew about stayed within fairly tight self-selected boundaries across the board: age, race, class, sexuality, education, even in the styles of clothing worn by members. The diversity of Heterodoxy was what surprised me most—an uncomfortable revelation to me. The more I learned about Heterodoxy, the more I began to see just how many limitations I had unconsciously accepted in many women's organizations.

As I continued to turn the pages of the album, thumbing through it again and again (with great care to avoid damaging the fragile pages), I was struck also by the number of well-known women who belonged. I had known from my readings in women's and social history that a few of these women had met or worked on similar political issues. Still, I had not realized that so many politically powerful women from early twentieth century American history not only knew each other, but dined together for years in a fairly intimate setting. They discussed the issues they were involved in, argued together, and learned much from each other's personal and political experiences. But somehow, in my reading of American women's history, I had seen each individual as if she were working in isolation from most other women, particularly if she were the first in her field, or involved in political movements or struggles outside the suffrage movement. The emphasis in the books I had read seemed to be on the men with whom she interacted, not the women who may have sustained or influenced her.

Also, in several years of reading histories and biographies (rather than *autobiographies*), I had never heard of Heterodoxy. For all the fame of some of its individual members, Heterodoxy barely rated a mention or footnote in modern published sources. Some of the Heterodoxy members who intrigued me the most were as unfamiliar as the club itself. One example was Marie Jenney Howe, the founder and guiding spirit behind the club's early success. She had slipped into oblivion, unknown and unremembered, along with many other members whose names and faces were new to me. It was as if they had disappeared without a trace—not an unusual fate for women, but damnably aggravating none-the-less.

So, that is how the great Heterodoxy search began. Since 1976, I have been a possessed woman, haunted by the elusive task of discovering and uncovering as much as I could about Heterodoxy itself, its founder Marie Jenney Howe, and the rest of the unknown or little-known members. Along the way, I have examined most of the published biographical sources relating to the 110 known club members, as well as several manuscript collections of more well-known individual Heterodites (as they called themselves). Of the manuscript collections, the most helpful have been the Inez Haynes Irwin Papers at the Schlesinger Library at Radcliffe College, where the "Heterodoxy to Marie" photograph album is located, and the La Follette Family Papers at the Library of Congress. The album was given as a gift of appreciation to Marie Jenney Howe on Christmas, 1920, and contains photographs of sixty members, complete with an often revealing statement or poem beneath the image of many members.[2] The album appears to have been added to at a later date, which makes it difficult to tell exactly which are the original photographs and entries and which are the additions (although clothing and hat styles as well as external evidence from other sources have helped a bit). Inez Haynes Irwin's papers also contain an unpublished and undated autobiography in typescript, which has an eleven-page section on Heterodoxy meetings as well as information on many of the club members. In fact, Irwin seems to have been a sort of unofficial club historian, which would explain how the album given to Howe came to be included in Irwin's papers after Howe's death. (Marie Jenney Howe's main body of papers have not yet been found, if they still exist. A very few of her letters are scattered in other Heterodoxy member's manuscript collections around the country.)

Also in the Irwin Papers are bound volumes of two magazines published by individual members: *Judy, A Magazine*, started by Anne Herendeen in June, 1919 with the editorial policy that *Judy* "will be pro-woman without being anti-man."[3] It lasted only three issues. By far more significant was Charlotte Perkins Gilman's *The Forerunner* (1909-1916), a sometimes brilliant, always thought-provoking feminist magazine. These magazines, plus the the Greenwich Village periodicals *The Masses* (1911-1917) and *The Quill* (1917-1926), proved to be invaluable records of articles written by various Heterodoxy members, while also providing a general overview of the beliefs and interests of many of the Heterodites.

Finally, Inez Irwin's papers contain a charming and unique spoof by Florence Guy Woolston (nee Seabury) of Elsie Clews Parsons' sociological study on *The Family*.[4] Both women belonged to Heterodoxy. The spoof was sort of an "in" joke among the Heterodites, entitled "Marriage Customs and Taboos Among the Early Heterodites." A complete copy is included here in Appendix A.

The La Follette Family Papers contain voluminous letters and documents concerning Fola La Follette, as well as La Follette family friend and lawyer Gilbert E. Roe and Heterodoxy member Gwyneth Roe. In searching these papers, I first discovered several letters in Marie Jenney Howe's own handwriting. The letters were very revealing about her feelings on religion, Heterodoxy, her relationships with her husband and with other club members. I was especially pleased to find several letters to Fola La Follette from other Heterodites describing Marie Howe's last days, death and her memorial service organized by Heterodoxy.

While these manuscript collections and others were extremely helpful, I feel sure that future researchers will be able to uncover more valuable information in as yet untapped sources. Although I collected every scrap of information that came my way, my main focus throughout has been to find material on the personal, professional, and political lives of members which would establish how these women might have been seen by their society as "unorthodox." That original focus has widened over the last ten years to include the value of Heterodoxy in their lives and the friendships gained through long association in the club. I have also tried to uncover some of the smaller, more telling stories from these women's lives which will illuminate their contributions to American history, as women who tried to do what they could to break the tight boundaries American society tried to force them to live within. And I have tried to discover how their association with each other in Heterodoxy influenced each woman's political beliefs and actions.

Finding the Heterodoxy album changed my life. As a child born with "slight" Cerebral Palsy, I spent too much of my childhood in hospitals and physical therapy clinics. My mother taught me to fight the limitations of my own body, as well as other people's prejudices against those who differ from them. I also fought those voices from childhood telling me that because my brain was damaged at birth, I was mentally retarded. Those same voices told me that because my body is somewhat different from the norm, caused by "birth defects," I am somehow "defective." I did not go to college immediately after high school, because, deep inside, those voices were still too strong to overcome. I went to work as a negative cutter, print inspector and later, color printer in photofinishing plants (including ten years at the San Francisco Technicolor plant), inspecting and/or printing over a thousand images per night shift. It is no wonder that a photograph album was to affect me so strongly and cause me to write my first book. I also owe my strong interest in lesbian history to the teachings of my Technicolor co-workers, who passed on their oral history along the assembly belt, in the "ladies' room," and around the dingy lunchroom tables during the long shifts. They spoke to my young eager ears and heart of love, isolation, oppression, military witchhunts, resistance, sexuality, suicide, and alienation (that word so evocative of being an "alien" sexual minority in a life-threatening heterosexual majority culture).

When I came out in 1964, I immediately joined the Daughters of Bilitis, the first organization for lesbians in the world, which luckily had its headquarters in San Francisco. It was so clear to me from the beginning that I could not bear to live my life in such isolation and oppression without support; nearly as clear as the feeling of enormous relief to discover that I, too, was a lesbian. Two of DOB's founders, Del Martin and Phyllis Lyon, were still deeply involved in the group. Off and on through the frantic 1960s and early 1970s, I went to meetings, softball games, discussions, rap groups, dances, social events, birthday parties, protest rallies, marches, and eventually presided over meetings and discussion groups held in my flat. I worked with others in organizing the DOB paperback library (an excellent training ground for my present work with the Lesbian Herstory Archives). On a couple of rare occasions I answered the phone calls to Daughters of Bilitis from rural and small town lesbians throughout the country who were living in intolerable isolation and despair, asking for information and encouragement to continue their lives. This, really, was my earliest education, along with "pillow talks" with my lover, Maryanne. She was twelve years older, which meant she had lesbian friends and former lovers who had first come out as far back as the 1930s. They, in turn, sometimes passed on to her the stories of other lesbians they had known and sometimes loved, who had lived as lesbians in an even earlier period of time. (This, my friends, is truly oral history!)

By my late twenties, when my self-confidence bloomed enough to allow me the courage to try college, I already knew that I wanted to study the hidden history of lesbians and gay men, as well as the neglected history of the so-called "average" person. But my first college history classes were almost unendurably boring recitations of white male history, taught by white men patting themselves on the back for the wars they had won, the countries they had conquered, the people they had enslaved. I learned the history of the oppressors and society's ideas of winners. It was not until my second year of college, when the first Women's Studies history class was taught at San Francisco City College, that I realized what it was I wanted to learn. I was looking for a way to fill in the background on all those women's stories passed down to my eager ears: the ones I heard on my grandmother's porch swing listening to her and her friends, sleepily shucking peas to the hum of their voices; the stories from the Army hospital's children's ward, where the weary mothers seldom realized their own bravery as they did what they could to help their disabled or sick children; the late night tales told in bits and pieces by my fellow prisoners in the Mobile, Alabama County Jail in 1959, where I spent the longest month of my life as a runaway at age sixteen; the stories of U.S. servicewomen and civilians stationed in Ankara, Turkey, where I graduated from high school; "how I got here" stories passed from woman to woman in the Florence Crittington Unwed Mothers' Home in Norfolk, Virginia, where I first fell in love with the woman who shared my "pre-mother's" room; and, of course, the tidbits of women's lives gleaned across the conveyor belt at Technicolor and during the "gab and java" Daughters of Bilitis discussion groups. I as well as others have been called "Pollyannas" for not giving in to despair when any smart person certainly would, but it wasn't for lack of brains that we did not see how bad things really were. Life has never been exactly simple for me, for my friends, for lesbians and gay men, and humanity in general in this strange world human beings have created. Three traits kept me going, and have fueled my research as well as my life: being an optimist and having a sense of humor, as well as an unquenchable curiosity to see how my life, their stories, and all the rest of it will turn out.

I went on to take every American Studies and women's history class I could, grateful that these classes came into being by the time I entered college. This book began life as my master's thesis in Women's Studies/Social Science at San Jose State University in 1977. Dr. Billie Jensen and Dr. Barbara Joans of the Women's Studies Program were unfailing book will encourage you to search out more of the sources listed in the bibliography. And if you find anything new, please let me know. This may be the last revised edition of *Radical Feminists of Heterodoxy*, but Heterodoxy will, undoubtedly, be a part of me the rest of my life.[6] (I guess now I'll just have to get started on the video documentary, or maybe a musical version.) I hope these women of Heterodoxy capture your imagination as they did mine.

Footnotes to Preface

1. "Heterodoxy to Marie," club photograph album, Christmas 1920, Inez Haynes Irwin Papers, Schlesinger Library, Radcliffe College, Cambridge, Massachusetts.
2. A biographical list of the members, including birth and death dates, occupations, political activities, and relationships, can be found in Appendix C.
3. *Judy, A Magazine*, June 1919, p. 3.
4. Elsie Clews Parsons, *The Family* (New York: G.P. Putnam, Sons, 1906).
5. The slideshow, "Women Who Did Things and Did Them Openly," is available for rent, purchase, or to set up a slideshow/lecture for Women's History, American Studies, and political science classes, or for fundraising and educational purposes by community, women's, lesbian and/or gay groups. Write me for more information c/o Lesbian Herstory Educational Foundation, Inc., P.O. Box 1258, New York, New York, 10116.
6. If anyone is interested in starting a Heterodoxy newsletter (a short, letter-style newsy thing, not a big production number), please get in touch with me. Researchers and readers pursuing individual Heterodites, Greenwich Village history and other aspects of Heterodoxy need a way to get in touch with each other and share their findings.

Introduction

"There was a club called Heterodoxy for unorthodox women," Mabel Dodge Luhan wrote in her autobiography, "women who did things and did them openly."[1] Elizabeth Gurley Flynn referred to her membership in Heterodoxy as "an experience of unbroken delight to me!" She added, "It has been a glimpse of the women of the future, big spirited, intellectually alert, devoid of the old 'femininity' which has been replaced by a wonderful freemasonry of women."[2]

In a 1920 album given to Heterodoxy founder Marie Jenney Howe by club members, one woman spoke for many when she wrote, "I'm so profoundly grateful for Heterodoxy . . . and so overwhelmingly glad that Heterodoxy is going to exist as long as we do, that there's nothing in lighter vein to say."[3] Other members made a point of writing about Heterodoxy's importance in their lives when they published their autobiographies, while often omitting other organizations they had joined. Their collective memories of Heterodoxy meetings conjure up images of often uproarious gatherings just this side of bedlam, the air filled with smoke, witty jibes and hotly debated political opinions tossed back and forth, with only Marie Jenney Howe's well-used gavel to rap a sense of order back into their Saturday luncheons.

This unique luncheon club for "unorthodox women" flourished in Greenwich Village in New York City from 1912 to the early years of World War II, meeting every other week except during the summer. The club's membership was drawn from women living primarily in three distinctive New York City neighborhoods: Greenwich Village, the Lower East Side, and Harlem. Yet it was not unusual for a good percentage of the members to be traveling or temporarily living in such disparate places as Wisconsin, Connecticut, New Mexico, China, Europe or Russia when a meeting took place. Heterodoxy was a haven for women of widely divergent political views, from Mary Logan Tucker, a staunch Republican, to Stella Cominsky Ballantine, niece of anarchist Emma Goldman who agreed with her aunt's politics; from admirers of the Progressive Party such as Senator Robert La Follette's daughter Fola, Marie Jenney Howe, and Netha Roe, to the Socialists Katharine Anthony, Elizabeth Gurley Flynn and Rose Pastor Stokes (with Flynn and Stokes becoming early members of the American Communist Party); and from Crystal Eastman's pacifist group, the American Union Against Militarism to military advocates and anti-pacifists Mary Logan Tucker of the Navy League and Rheta Childe Dorr.

The personal and sexual lives of the women in the club were as widely varied as their political views. Conventionally married heterosexual women traded childrearing tips with Elisabeth Irwin, who was raising several adopted children with the help of her lover, Katharine Anthony. Several women kept their maiden names after marriage, no light matter so early in the twentieth century. Some of the members had been through scandalous divorces, while others were forceful advocates of women's right to free love outside the confines of conventional marriage. Many members never married a man, although at least two lesbian couples referred to their relationships in marriage terms. At least twelve Heterodites were not in the least heterosexual, while others enjoyed sexual and romantic relationships with both sexes. All of Heterodoxy's members were ardently pro-women supporters who knew the vital necessity of strong female friendships as well as the importance of sharing information with other women outside the narrow confines of friendship circles.

Professionally, Heterodoxy covered a wide field of occupations: authors, lawyers, journalists, stockbrokers, theatrical managers and directors, physicians, playwrights, social reformers, actresses, educators, psychologists, and, eventually, radio commentators and motion picture scriptwriters. Many of these women—particularly the original group of charter members, most of whom had begun their careers before 1900—educated themselves for professions long before it was considered commonplace for women. More than a few Heterodites were economically independent through their own efforts and earnings; relatively few relied on their husband's money or inherited income to support themselves or their children.

American women had, of course, gathered together into clubs and organizations before the twentieth century, beginning with groups such as the Female Society for the Relief and Employment of the Poor in 1798. By the end of the nineteenth century, cultural circles, ladies's library associations, and other women's clubs had become widespread and numerous. The nation-wide General Federation of Women's Clubs was formed in 1889 to give cohesion to women's civic and cultural efforts. Previous attempts at national organizations for women had focused primarily on women's interest in religious and benevolent work (under such groups as the Women's Home Mission Board (1877)), and their desire to diminish the sale of liquor (through the united efforts of the Women's Christian Temperance Union (1874)). The growing demand for woman's suffrage began before the Civil War, and captured the energy and loyalty of legions of women soon afterwards. By 1890 the movement was represented by the merger of two earlier rival organizations into the National American Woman Suffrage Association.[4] All of these associations, self-improvement circles, and women's clubs had a unifying factor, however—an interest, a cause, a belief (even if only in their own city or town) which formed a center around which the individual members could gather into a more or less cohesive unit.

On the surface, Heterodoxy appears to lack a central belief or reason for existence (other than being "unorthodox" women). In fact, the members took great pride in their diverse personalities and unusual range of interests. When I first learned of this club's existence, I wondered how it was possible that the only unpleasant incident members could later recall throughout the hectic years of Heterodoxy—the Progressive Era of the 1910s, the First World War, the frantic 1920s, through the Depression—centered around the issue of political differences and pacifism during the War. [Since the first edition was published, new evidence from the 1920s has revealed a less rosy picture, yet no less fascinating. See Chapter 4, "Heterodoxy and Politics".] As I read the warm, witty and touching comments under each member's photograph in the 1920 album, I found myself asking how Heterodoxy, which met only once very two weeks for lunch, a speech and talking among themselves, could become as important as it obviously was in their lives. Was Heterodoxy really only a social gathering place for liberal and radical women, or did it have political implications and private effects not readily noticeable on the surface?

Anyone intrigued with the club who reads Lois Banner's textbook *Women in Modern America* [5] would think Heterodoxy was little more than a coffee-klatch for half-crazed mystics. After discussing Heterodoxy member Henrietta Rodman's Feminist Alliance group in New York's Greenwhich Village of the 1910s, Banner states that Heterodoxy:

> . . .was even less inclined toward activism than the Feminist Alliance. Its members included many of the leading women of the day. . . .. They met to discuss their common problems and to give and gain mutual support. One observer, after attending a meeting of Heterodoxy, wrote that they seemed to be "in church," that they were worshipping at some holy shrine, their voices and their eyes were full of religious excitement. [6]

Banner took that misleading and condescending quote out of context from Hutchins Hapgood's aptly titled autobiography, *A Victorian in the Modern World*.[7] Hapgood was supposedly quoting the dancer Elsie Dufour, a Heterodoxy member who was not describing a Heterodoxy meeting, but merely members' reactions to Susan Glaspell's new play *The Verge*, one of the first feminist plays they had seen. The Heterodites had good reason to be excited, particularly since so many Heterodoxy women were so deeply involved in the theater.

Hapgood's memory of Elsie Dufour's comments twenty years after the fact may have been colored by his feelings about the "almost insane atmosphere" of ideas and beliefs of the feminists he knew. The journalist Hapgood was horrified by Heterodoxy members, "women of character and personal charm and beauty," who, though they "had their husbands and lovers like other women, yet felt that in so doing they were merely gratifying some of their commonplace instincts."[8] Like many of the professed "male feminists" and companions of the "new woman" of his day, Hapgood was a die-hard romantic. While clearly enjoying the sexual advantages of bedding the free-love feminists in Greenwich Village, he feared the shifting power of the new male-female relationships while giving lip service to the justice of equal suffrage for women. It is hard to understand why Banner chose to quote him as her only source on Heterodoxy, when so many members published books containing their accounts of the club.[9] It is past time that we hear the women's version of Heterodoxy, and let Hapgood's go to the oblivion it deserves.

Far better for us to recall that even in the last decade of the club's existence, Heterodite Mary Ware Dennett wrote Netha Roe that she had joined forces with yet another political group:

Yes! The Union Idea Now comes first. I am increasingly for it. I tried not to be interested in it, having become so weary with organizations and movements and causes, and so sceptical wherewithal. But it got to me, gradually but surely. . . .

Heterodoxy? Well, it has gone along this year with a revolving system of chairmanship, a different one at each meeting and meetings once a month. It has worked very well; not that *all* the old atmosphere is evident all the time, but on the whole, it had been fine, —a pleasure that is unique, and for which there is no substitute that I know of. We have missed you heaps.[10]

Both women were in their seventies when this letter was written in 1940; they had both belonged to Heterodoxy for twenty-eight years. Yet Mary Ware Dennett's political activism and loving support of her sister Heterodite are as clear as they were when the Heterodoxy club album was put together in 1920. In letters and in diaries, the last surviving members continued to proclaim Heterodoxy's unique place in their lives literally to their dying days. Is it any wonder that a growing band of Heterodite lovers have taken up the search through dusty cubby holes in bookstores and archives for every scrap of information about this "little band of wilful [sic] women, the most unruly and individualistic females you ever fell among"?

Maule, Frances

4

Footnotes to Introduction

1. Mabel Dodge Luhan, *Intimate Memories,* Vol. III: *Movers and Shakers* (New York: Harcourt, Brace & Co., 1936), p. 143.
2. Elizabeth Gurley Flynn, "Heterodoxy to Marie," club gift album to Marie Jenny Howe, Christmas 1920, Inez Haynes Irwin Papers, Arthur and Elizabeth Schlesinger Library.
3. Netha Roe, "Heterodoxy to Marie" club album.
4. *Encyclopedia of the Social Sciences,* 1934 edition, s.v. "Women's Organizations" by Gladys Meyerand. For a more recent feminist analysis of organized women, see Karen J. Blair, *The Clubwoman as Feminist: True Womanhood Redefined, 1864-1914* (New York: Holmes & Meier, 1980).
5. Lois Banner, *Women in Modern America,* (New York: Harcourt Brace Jovanovich, 1974).
6. Ibid., p. 108.
7. Hutchins Hapgood, *A Victorian in the Modern World,* (New York: Harcourt, 1939).
8. Ibid.
9. Banner's choice of Hapgood's quote is especially unfortunate since *Women in Modern America* is an important feminist sourcebook for women's history, and her use of Hapgood's quote implies agreement. Elaine Showalter's introduction to the excellent *These Modern Women: Autobiographical Essays from the Twenties* (Old Westbury, NY: Feminist Press, 1978) states that Heterodoxy meetings were "intensely feminist and emotional" (p. 7). The only source listed for her conclusion is Hapgood's quote in Banner's book. This is a good example of how questionable sources are given new life and eventually become established "fact."
10. Mary Ware Dennett to Netha Roe, March 28, 1940, La Follette Family Papers, Library of Congress.

Marie Jenny and friend

Marie Jenney Howe

"...Undoubtedly the keystone holding us together..."[1]

Marie Jenney Howe was the Mother of Heterodoxy in the best meaning of that term. She created the club in 1912; nurtured the women who came to the meetings emotionally, intellectually and politically while delighting in the individuality of their distinct personalities; strengthened individual self-worth for those members who needed it; and guided the club and its members with a firm, fair hand over the rough spots through the club's long history. She wanted a place where women of "unorthodox" opinions could gather, talk with each other, and hear about their childhoods, daily lives, interests and beliefs. She hoped it would be a setting where social constraints and conventional politeness were outweighed by the sheer delight in honest disagreement and differences which opened the mind to new possibilities, new ways of thinking, living, being. When she moved to New York City and couldn't find an organization quite like what she had in mind, Marie Howe simply decided to start a new group to fit what she needed for herself. With the creation of Heterodoxy, she formed a nourishing atmosphere of stimulating talk, great rollicking laughter, and a sharing among the women of the pain and pleasures in being activists of diverse interests. It worked. The reason it worked had a lot to do with the background, multiple interests and personality of Marie Jenney Howe.

Marie Jenney was born December 26, 1870, in Syracuse, New York, one of Marie Saul and Edwin Sherman Jenney's three children. Her parents were from prosperous old New York families. Marie attended Dobbs Ferry Elementary School and was very close to her mother. She grew into a striking young woman with large, warm brown eyes, thick brown hair, and a strong character. It is unclear whether she suffered in her youth from the heart ailments that plagued her later life, or whether she had another, less permanent illness. However, in an early informal photograph in the "Heterodoxy to Marie" 1920 album, Marie sits in an overstuffed easy chair, her hand lingering on the neck of her guitar, her head leaning upon small satin pillows while her feet rest on foot pillows covered with animal skins. A handwritten caption labels the image "A Long Time Ago when She was an Invalid for Two Years." Marie wears a loose gown and robe. A properly attired, stiff-backed woman friend sits facing away from the camera. The curtains are drawn. Marie Jenney's face is listless, maybe even a little bored, as she listens to her friend reading to her over the china tea cups. Even the unusual event of a cumbersome camera recording the homey, overcrowded scene does not seem to rouse her interest. Can this be the same woman who decades later physically pulled writer Fannie Hurst out of a roaring crowd to help hold a women's suffrage banner in the 1912 Fifth Avenue parade?

Whatever the cause, something kept Marie Jenney from entering Union Theological Seminary in Meadville, Pennsylvania until 1893 when she was twenty-two years old. Considering the evidence that she felt a strong vocation towards the ministry, one wonders whether her illness or family opposition forced her to delay her studies. It is possible that she had to convince her father to pay for a career-oriented education. He may have agreed with the townspeople of Meadville, who "insisted that she could not be serious."[2] Rumor had it that Marie Jenney could only be in Meadville because of a secret involvement with a male student.

> There were other women studying at the school, but Miss Jenney was different. She was too beautiful to be a minister. . . . Only a man could explain such a beautiful girl . . . at a theological seminary. Women did not go in for careers . . . and saving souls was a man's job. It seemed absurd for her to go into the ministry.[3]

The young law student Frederic C. Howe agreed with the townspeople completely when he returned home to Meadville for a visit and first saw Marie Jenney. Frustrated by her indifference to him during dinner at the home of mutual friends, Fred Howe wondered "Why should such a woman . . . be studying Hebrew, Greek, and the early church fathers? It was all very stupid. I had never heard of such a thing." Their first conversation was a disaster from Fred's point of view. This is hardly surprising, when he stated in his autobiography that he believed at the time that "all girls got married if they could; certainly all good-looking girls did."[4] Twenty-five year old Fred chose to begin his courtship of Marie with the strange tactic of anti-women comments. He recalled later:

> I quoted a remark of Heine that every woman who did anything in the world had one eye on her work and the other eye on a man. The only exception was Countess Somebody or Other, but then she had only one eye. The joke failed miserably. I endeavored to bolster it up by saying that Johns Hopkins [his university] did not admit women and that I hoped it never would. . . .The afternoon was a dismal failure. She seemed quite willing to see me go.[5]

Actually, one wonders why Marie Jenney continued to speak to him at all after that conversation, but she did. Frederic Howe put to good use his lifelong trait of tenacity in the face of overwhelming disapproval. He courted Marie as often and as ardently as she would allow, buying books to discuss economics with her and arranging picnics and walks. Marie Jenney was probably drawn to spend time in his company by Fred's intelligent and passionate (if often ill-informed) discussion of political topics, as well as the thought that here was a worthy foe with whom to test her debating skills on women's rights and other issues.

Much of the time they spent together, Fred Howe was mercifully silent, pondering Marie's committment to her vocation and the arguments she presented on behalf of women. [It was just as well: every time he opened his mouth, he put both feet in it.] In his autobiography, Howe was frank in recalling his reluctance to give up his traditional views on a woman's "place." "In so far as I thought of it at all, women were conveniences of men. Mothers were, sisters were, wives would be," Howe declared. "Men were kind to them,"[6] much as any well-bred man would be to a good dog. In other words, Howe was typical of the men of his era.

He was disturbed by Marie Jenney's ideas and mental independence as much as he was attracted by her beauty and intelligence. She boldly disagreed with much that he took for granted, and backed her opinions with sound reasoning.

> Miss Jenney was different . . . I expected women to agree; she had ideas of her own; they were better than my own, more logical, more consistent too with my democratic ideas on other things. She believed that women should vote for the same reasons that men voted. I snorted at the idea. . . . Women, to her, should be economically independent, they should not be compelled to ask for money, they should have an allowance; they did their share of the common work, and marriage was a partnership. . . . To her, life was not a man's thing, it was a human thing. It was to be enjoyed by women as it was by men; there should be equality in all things, not in the ballot alone but in the mind, in work, in a career. Men and women were different in some ways; they were alike in more.[7]

Howe tried to steer their conversations away from the dangerous topics of sexual equality and women's rights, since they "were disagreeable; when we were married there would be time enough to discuss such questions."[8] His ego assured him that despite their total disagreement on many issues, Marie Jenney would surely accept his proposal. Before he left Meadville, Frederic Howe tried to put their tentative relationship on firmer ground. However, Marie Jenney reminded him again, as she had so many times before, that she intended to become a minister as soon as she graduated. Fred was surprised when Marie told him that "she wanted her career; she wanted to do something for the world. She loved her work and I hated mine." When they parted, Marie agreed to exchange letters with Fred. "My letters alternated hope and despair," Fred Howe recalled. "Hers were full of the work she planned to do."[9]

In 1897, Marie Jenney graduated from the Seminary and left Meadville for her first position as an assistant to the renowned Rev. Mary A. Safford in Sioux City, Iowa. The following June, Rev. Safford was one of three women ministers who officiated at Marie Jenney's ordination in her home town of Syracuse. Mary Safford was a popular woman's suffrage speaker and president of the Iowa Suffrage Association, as well as a strong advocate for women ministers in the Unitarian Church. From 1899 to 1904, Marie Jenney assisted Rev. Safford in ministering to the First Unitarian Church in Des Moines, Iowa. There, she concentrated on building the congregation and the daily needs of the church and membership, while Rev. Safford traveled and preached throughout Iowa. Rev. Marie Jenney became widely known as the popular "Little Minister," respected for her own growing leadership abilities and warm personality.[10]

In the meantime, Frederic Howe matured into an idealistic lawyer with a social conscience and a strong belief in Progressive politics. He worked as an activist Cleveland municipal reformer under Mayor Tom L. Johnson, who was an innovative mayor much respected for his political courage and honesty. The letters Rev. Jenney and the reforming lawyer exchanged for seven years, as well as a growing sense of shared purpose and political interests appear to have helped ripen the dormant romantic friendship. Rev. Marie Jenney, aged thirty-three, married Frederic Howe in 1904. Perhaps if and when their letters are found, they will help us understand why independent Rev. Jenney not only agreed to marry after seven years of the ministry, but also why she felt compelled to give up her career as a Unitarian minister on her wedding day. It was true that Fred seemed to have changed his mind at last about women's rights and liberalized his views on other social issues, but some of those changes were only surface deep. "Honest to an unusual degree," Fred Howe was considered by Hutchins Hapgood as "kindness itself, but his was a kindness that didn't enter deeply into the instincts. He was capable of great affection, but he held himself aloof from the passions of human beings."[11] Later, in his autobiography, Howe showed how honest he could be:

> As to women, I followed the changing mores. I spoke for women's suffrage without much wanting it. And I urged freedom for women without liking it. My mind gave way, but not my instincts. . . . I hated privilege in the world of economics; I chose it in my own home.
>
> And I have sometimes doubted whether many of the men who spoke and worked for the equality of women really desired it. Intellecutually yes, but instinctively, no; they clung as did I to the propertied instinct, to economic supremacy, to the old idea of marriage, in which all that a woman got she got through petitioning for it.[12]

Whatever Marie Jenney expected from her marriage to the kindly but dispassionate Fred, she seems to have been sadly disappointed. Although their marriage lasted (at least in name) until her death, they never had children. Marie's few letters which have been found are warm, witty and charming until Fred is mentioned. Then, it is as if an emotional curtain is drawn over a disappointing domestic drama, even when she was writing to her most intimate friends. Fred was not honored by an inscription in the two books about George Sand which Marie wrote. Instead, one was dedicated to her young friend, Fola La Follette, while *George Sand: The Search for Love* bears a dedication to Marie's most beloved friend and possible lover, Rose Young. Both women were among the earliest members of Heterodoxy. The observant, if sometimes unreliable, Hutchins Hapgood saw Marie Jenney Howe as

> a woman of very strong mental and emotional character, and one also endowed to an extraordinary degree with what we call femininity, caring more for love and affection even than most women, yet thoroughly impregnated with the feeling that there was a conspiracy of men against women. It was a feeling characteristic of that

time. . . . Fred was, however, dominantly a mental person. . . . He couldn't understand Marie's deep unconscious needs, and she could not understand how he could be so good and kind and yet so aloof. In some way, I think she mistakenly felt that this, too, had to do with man's inhumanity to woman.[13]

According to Howe's own words in his autobiography about his lukewarm feelings on women, Marie Jenney Howe was *not* mistaken.

After her marriage, Rev. Howe never served as a minister again, other than to officiate at the marriages and funerals of friends. Why did she give up her career on her wedding day? Fred Howe would have us believe that Marie Jenney accepted without any inner struggle the traditional role of non-working wife, although he does admit that he "unconsciously" put up psychological barriers within the marriage against any "wife of his" making him look like a man who "couldn't support his wife." However, I think it likely that she had decided to leave the ministry whether she married Fred Howe or not. Evidence in two references from the end of her life show that she had a crisis of faith. A year before she died, Marie Jenney Howe wrote to her dear friend Fola La Follette:

> What troubles me more than anything is that I wish there was a God. I want a Something, a Someone. I can't get over it. That's childishness I suppose, or what is called the religious temperament.[14]

At her memorial service, tributes to her memory called her "a person who found through the ministry that churches were not necessarily close to God, and who thereafter embarked on an extensive search. . . ."[15] Perhaps when more information comes to light about her years as a minister, it will clear up the mystery of what could have happened during those seven years that made marriage to Fred Howe more appealing than life as a minister.

After her marriage, Marie continued her work for women's suffrage in Cleveland, Ohio, her new hometown. She also became involved in local political issues, and was credited with converting Mayor Tom L. Johnson from a gentlemanly traditionalist who saw all women as ladies in need of protection, into a strong supporter and public speaker for equal suffrage.[16]

The Howes became close friends and supporters of Wisconsin Senator Robert La Follette and his family after Fred Howe met La Follette in 1907.[17] La Follette's Progressive politics appealed to Fred and Marie, with its advocacy of Henry George's single tax on land values, municipal improvements, child labor laws and regulation of food and drugs. Marie Jenney Howe joined the new National Consumer's League, which attempted to combine consumer buying and boycotting pressure with government legislation to change the working conditions of women and children. Her organizational abilities gained her the presidency of the Ohio Consumer's League and vice-presidency of the National Consumer's League before the Howes moved from Cleveland to New York City in 1910.

New York City in 1910! Was there ever such a place before or since?

Marie Jenny Howe

The historical image that comes to mind is of a rich ethnic, cultural and racial polyglot mixture of peoples; an exciting visual juxtaposition of the first skyscrapers built alongside the lowliest squalid tenements. Its vast media resources focused strongly on the happenings of "The City" over all other cities and assured New York a unique place in America's collective consciousness, so that the smallest child growing up anywhere else hungered to see it while fearing its evil ways. New York was at that time the very essence of an American city, with the exceptionally wealthy and the prosperous middle-class showing only minimal concern for workers who barely had enough to eat. Most (but certainly not all) New Yorkers truly believed in the magic word "opportunity." Present-day New Yorkers are far more historically aware of the city's rich cultural and historical past than New York residents of the early 1900s. Then, New Yorkers were too busy coping with the rapid changes in their world to know or care much about the city's past. The future was paramount, with most residents concentrating on personal dreams of a better future. Even the poorest inhabitants found enjoyment, as well as pain, in freedom from old cultural ways that smaller, more family-bound communities could not offer. Anything could happen in a place like New York, and everything did.

Elisabeth Irwin

Katharine Anthony

Temporarily settled in the legendary Chelsea Hotel, Marie Jenney Howe plunged into the New York Suffrage movement, rapidly becoming the chair of the Twenty-Fifth Assembly District division of the New York City Woman Suffrage Party (part of the National American Woman Suffrage Association); her district soon became known as "the Fighting Twenty-Fifth" under her dynamic leadership. She also helped form and was an early vice-president of the New York State Suffrage League. During one of the earliest suffrage parades in New York, Marie Jenney Howe met a future Heterodoxy member, author Fannie Hurst. Hurst recalled:

> One Saturday afternoon, as I was walking down Fifth Avenue, I ran bang into one of the suffrage celebrations. Phalanzes [sic] of women swung up the street, their banners proclaiming. . . . Next thing I knew, I was in formation, marching up the Avenue, and helping my neighbor clutch the pole of a banner which read: "Move Over, Gentlemen. We Have Come to Stay." . . . The woman with whom I shared the heavy pole was a brilliant-eyed, dark-haired mite who introduced herself, Marie Jenney Howe. Marching in the phalanx of men, I was later to discover, was her husband, Fred Howe.[18]

Not long after arriving in New York, the Howes moved into an apartment on West Twelfth Street "on the edge of Greenwich Village," where they "began in earnest our New York life." They both became deeply involved in the hectic Bohemian spirit of their new neighborhood. Fred recalled that "brilliant young people, full of vitality, ardent about saving the world, floated in and out of our apartment."[19]

Among their new friends and neighbors were the young lawyer and social activist Crystal Eastman and her brother Max, who were among the group that edited and published *The Masses*, a radical social protest periodical; Ruth Hale, who married the journalist Heywood Broun and then started the Lucy Stone League in support of married women who preferred to keep their maiden names; the educator, free spirit, and sometime nudist Henrietta Rodman, founder of the Feminist Alliance in defense of married teachers in the New York public school system and organizer of the Village branch of the Liberal Club; and the progressive educator Elisabeth Irwin, founder of the Little Red Schoolhouse, and her lifelong lover and partner, social researcher and feminist biographer Katharine Anthony. Many more famous, infamous and extraordinary "average" women who lived in or passed through New York would later be drawn in as members, speakers, and/or guests of Heterodoxy. By the time Marie Jenney Howe conceived of the idea of a club for unorthodox women, she knew many who fit that description perfectly. Some were close allies in the woman suffrage cause, such as Mary Ware Dennett, Paula Jakobi, Claire Mumford, Inez Milholland, Rheta Childe Dorr, and Doris Stevens. More charter members were part of the Howe's Greenwich Village community, including the playwright Susan Glaspell, actress Virginia Kline, critic Nell Dawson, and the Freudian psychologist Grace Potter. Finally, Marie called upon some of her long-time friends in the Progressive Party to join the new organization, friends such as budding actress Fola La Follette, who had moved in with Marie and Fred Howe to pursue a career in the theater. Physical education instructor Gwyneth (Netha) Roe moved from Madison, Wisconsin with her husband, radical lawyer Gilbert Roe, just in time to become a charter member. Finally, novelist Edna Kenton was drawn into Heterodoxy through her political interests in suffrage, her friendship with Marie as well as her connections with the Provincetown Playhouse and Susan Glaspell.

What a rich cast of characters to draw upon! Yet these were only a few of the women brought together to form the nucleus of Heterodoxy's earliest years. Charlotte Perkins Gilman, another early member, described Marie Jenney Howe's intentions in forming Heterodoxy very well in her inscription to the 1920 album:

TO QUEEN MARIE

Who gathers folk of warring creed
And holds them all as friends,
Who ministers to social needs,
And strives for social ends—
All praise to her for her deed
And the great gift she spends.[20]

The Evening Sun, Tuesday February 17, 1914
(from Manuscript Division, Library of Congress)

Footnotes to Chapter 1

1. Elizabeth Gurley Flynn, "Heterodoxy to Marie" club album.
2. Frederic C. Howe, *The Confessions of a Reformer* (New York: Scribner, 1925), p. 65.
3. Ibid.
4. Ibid., pp. 65-66.
5. Ibid., p. 66.
6. Ibid., pp. 66-67.
7. Ibid., pp. 67-68.
8. Ibid.
9. Ibid., p. 69.
10. Clara Cook Helvie, *Unitarian Women Ministers* (Middleburg, Mass.: privately published, 1928); Catherine F. Hitchings, *Universalist and Unitarian Women Ministers* (NY: Universalist Historical Society, 1975).
11. Hapgood, p. 333.
12. Howe, pp. 234-235.
13. Hapgood, pp. 332-333.
14. Marie Jenney Howe to Fola La Follette, March 22, 1933, La Follette Family Papers.
15. *New York Times*, March 2, 1934, p. 22.
16. Howe, pp. 137-138.
17. Bella Case La Follette and Fola La Follette, *Robert La Follette*, 2 vols. (NY: Macmillan, 1953), 1:224.
18. Fannie Hurst, *Anatomy of Me*, (London, Jonathan Cape, 1959), p. 246.
19. Howe, p. 240.
20. Charlotte Perkins Gilman, "Heterodoxy to Marie" club album.

Newspaper clipping
1914
(Library of Congress)

Heterodoxy's Early Years

On summoning the charter members of Heterodoxy
She bade us think — but nothing USUAL!
It must be different
Though it may be dull.
I thought as hard and as often
As I could for one of my size
But it was never "different" enough![1]

Heterodoxy began in 1912 with an original group of twenty-five members. In the beginning the luncheon and debate meetings were held in Greenwich Village, probably at Polly Halliday's famous Mac-Dougall Street restaurant where the food was good and cheap, and the tables were long wooden trestles with benches. "The heart of Bohemia pulsed evenly and regularly at Polly's," and the artists, writers, socialists and anarchists who lived in the Village during the period from 1912 to 1920 considered the restaurant their neighborhood club, meeting place, and home away from home.[2] Since Henrietta Rodman was both the guiding force behind the Liberal Club and a charter Heterodoxy member, the Liberal Club's rooms above Polly's were probably made available on the alternate Saturdays when Heterodoxy met. Years later, the meetings and luncheons shifted to the Town Hall Club.

Membership dues in Heterodoxy were a minimal two dollars a year; the members paid for their luncheon at the table. Heterodoxy soon added new members to the original core group. They were often friends of the original members or other "unorthodox" women who were asked to join the club after attending a meeting, such as Elizabeth Gurley Flynn. By the creation of the club album in late 1920, the membership stood at sixty.

As this revised edition was about to go to press, researcher Patricia McC. Miller found the first known Heterodoxy membership list in her search through Helen Hull's papers still in the possession of her nephew, Frederick Hull. Undated, the list of eighty names and addresses seems to have been created between 1920 and 1922. Fola La Follette's address is listed as 20 Rue Jacob, Paris (Natalie Barney's home) where she and her husband George Middleton lived during those years. Six women on the list were unknown as Heterodoxy members before the list was found: Zelma C. Brandt, Bertha Carter, Daisy Chase, Eleanor Fitzgerald, Margaret Lane, and Leanora Speyer. Who they were, how they became members, and what their lives were like are still mysteries, as there has not been time enough to do more than the most minimal search for information. This exciting find confirms that members were still considered Heterodites whether they stayed in New York or lived in other parts of the world. Ellen La Motte's address was simply listed as "China," and Zona Gale's address was Wisconsin.[3]

17

Before the club disbanded in the early 1940s, Heterodoxy claimed a maximum number of one hundred and ten identifiable members. However, only thirty-five to fifty members attended most meetings. Inez Haynes Irwin's unpublished autobiography contains a detailed twelve-page section describing Heterodoxy. She stated that:

> Heterodoxy was the easiest of clubs. The meetings were almost invariably addressed by members. It entailed no duties or obligations. There was no press.[4]

Few clubs, either women's or men's, would have either desired or had need for such a ruling, but it becomes clear why Heterodoxy demanded "off the record" when one realizes how many of the members were either journalists, public speakers, actresses, or writers. In the days of the "penny dreadfull" and "yellow press" newspapers that sold reputations downriver every time one of their issues hit the stands, such public women were often misquoted and gossiped about in print. It must have been a delightful relief for them to find that they could speak freely whatever came to mind, without fear of the next morning's newspaper headlines. Still, I wish they hadn't kept their vows quite so well. When some good woman finally invents a time machine, my first desire is to become an invisible observer at a Saturday Heterodoxy meeting. Until then, or until someone finds that a member kept notes on the actual meetings, we will have to make do with the little information that has survived.

Considering how many of the 1920 album inscriptions refer to Marie Howe's talent for keeping order during the meetings, the meetings must have often resembled the Tower of Babel itself. Caroline Singer enjoyed Heterodoxy's:

> Loud talk and simple feasting: Discussion of philosophy,
> Investigation of subtleties. Tongues loosened
> And minds at one.
> Hearts refreshed
> By discharge of emotion[5]

Another member, Mary Chamberlain, wrote:

> Every Saturday I wish that it were "every other Saturday" so that I could sit at table with the rest of us and hear Marie keep all of us merry and witty and good—in spite of 59 varieties of temper, temperament and viewpoint.[6]

The strong-minded and verbal members surely *could* all "talk . . . argue . . . listen," but sometimes apparently, they forgot (or got too riled up) to do the listening part. Frances Maule toasted Marie Howe for making sense out of the chaos that often ensued:

> Here's to you, Marie—and may your gavel continue to rap the table at Heterodoxy luncheons with undiminished vigor in the years that are to come. Sooner would I that it fall on my knuckles or on my head than that its discipline should be removed from us.[7]

Alice Duer Miller put it more succinctly, calling Marie Howe:

> The only chairman I ever knew
> Who could make me do
> What I ought to do,
> Without a terrible hullaballoo![8]

Much as she enjoyed the "hullaballoo" of nimble minds at work, Marie Jenney Howe's legendary wit, resourcefulness and intelligence must have been put to the test many times keeping some of the Heterodoxy meetings just this side of bedlam. As chair, she had to dull the roar of the most vocal members without dulling the discussion as well.

Most importantly, Heterodoxy meetings served as an informal but valuable news source about the battle for women's rights and political issues, wherever they were being fought. Helen Keller, Margaret Sanger, Amy Lowell, Emma Goldman, Finnish peace advocate Mrs. Malmberg, and many other non-members spoke to the group. Members and non-members alike addressed Heterodoxy on vital international issues such as pacifism, birth control, the Russian Revolution as seen firsthand by Heterodoxy women, health issues, infant mortality, anarchism as a political tool for social change, education of women, Black civil rights, disabled women, the Irish independence movement, free love, psychology, and so much more. In fact, it seems that few topics affecting women throughout the world were overlooked.

Barbed wire + other entanglements on the Russian front.

Bessie Beatty

"What did Heterodoxy talk about? It talked about everything," Inez Haynes Irwin reminisced.

> Heterodoxy members came from many states of the Union. Most of them had traveled with amazing extensiveness. Among them were Democrats, Republicans, Socialists, anarchists, liberals and radicals of all opinions. They possessed minds startlingly free of prejudice. They were at home with ideas. All could talk; all could argue; all could listen. . . .Our occupations and preoccupations ranged the world. Many of our members were working for various reforms. A sizable proportion were always somewhere else. During the First World War, when no Americans were supposed to enter Russia, . . .at least two members of Heterodoxy were there writing articles.[9]

One of Marie Howe's innovations became the most popular feature of Heterodoxy meetings. She requested members to prepare a "background talk" on their lives as a means to draw the women closer together.

> A member told whatever she chose to reveal about her childhood, girlhood and young womanhood. They ranged in atmosphere from the middle-western farm on which Leta Hollingworth's childhood was spent, where all her dresses were made from flour bags which had the manufacturer's name printed on them, through a life of inherited rebelliousness, like that of Charlotte Perkins Gilman; from the cold, faded elegance of the great house on the Hudson, in which Alice Duer Miller was raised, to the fiery shadow of Emma Goldman, in which Stella Comen Ballantine (who was her niece and adoring partisan) lived. . .; from the gorgeous gusto of Lou Rogers' childhood, deep in the Maine country, to the quiet of Helen Hull's early life in the Middle West which was so like one of her own rich novels.[10]

Inez Irwin added: "I have never listened to such talks as those backgrounds." Well she might say that! Few people have. Yet those talks, along with the comments and questions afterwards by other Heterodoxy members, were early forerunners of consciousness-raising groups of the modern feminist movement. Their advantages and benefits were much the same as well, particularly in breaking down the isolation of women who were not only living in a large city of strangers, but more importantly, who had grown up as rebels in a world of more orthodox, ordinary people. Like those of us who have gone through consciousness-raising sessions in the more recent feminist movement, Heterodoxy women must have often been startled to discover that despite the differences in their backgrounds, most of them as children had received the same messages and expectations from their families and the society around them. Where, outside Heterodoxy, could these women find such a sympathetic and supportive audience for their "unorthodox" feelings, political beliefs and personal lives?

Among the few descriptions of Heterodoxy meetings uncovered thus far, one was of a "background talk" concerning childrearing practices. Inez Haynes Irwin described psychologist Leta Hollingworth's suggestion that the mothers among the members give talks on their children. Leta Hollingworth had been studying a class of highly intelligent children throughout their school careers for twenty years, and wanted to hear if her friends were raising their children differently than they had been reared by their parents. Inez Irwin recalled:

> Like Edna Kenton, like Katharine Anthony, Leta was a wise woman. . . .I remember that Daisy [Haynes Thompson], talking about [her daughter] Ebie who was born when [Daisy] was forty-four [said]: "Everything I have done for my child has been the wrong thing. I have made every mistake possible, but anyway she is a happy girl." How Leta . . . drank those talks down![11]

It may seem on the surface that talks by doting mothers about their children weren't exactly radical feminism. Yet in many cases, the mothers themselves were trying to raise their children in radically different

Leta Hollingworth

ways from the traditional upbringing of the time. Unfortunately, sometimes the old ways might have been better for all concerned, particularly the children. Ruth Hale's and Heywood Broun's strongly professed belief that all family members were perfectly equal created more problems than it solved for their son, Heywood Hale Broun. He writes of his childhood:

> . . .there was the question of government in the layered little kingdoms of Eighty-fifth Street. [Heywood lived on the first floor, Ruth Hale on the second floor, and their son on the third.] Ruth's and Heywood's floors were the domain of dictators who could keep the lights on as late as they liked. . . .
>
> Ruth and Heywood never seemed to realize how much they confused me with all their efforts at equality. The rigid, rule-filled households that had shadowed their early years were, in the case of their fortunate son, to be replaced with a kind of social democracy in which the sunshine of reason lit every corner and where discipline would lose its sting by being explained.[12]

Their son paid a high price in emotional confusion and pain for the unspoken, unallowed anger in the modern-era, psychology-conscious Hale-Broun household.

Another short reference describes a Heterodite's speech to the club. In 1919, Katharine Anthony wrote to a friend:

> At the Heterodoxy luncheon last Saturday, Zona Gale was present and she made a speech about the University of Wisconsin girls who were opposing sororities, and their experiences. I remembered that your daughter had a share in that and was pleased to think that their efforts were getting recognition so far away from the scene of action.[13]

One of the most amusing accounts of a Heterodoxy meeting was related by Dr. Sara Josephine Baker. She broke the "off-the-record" rule in her autobiography *Fighting For Life*, when she recounted poet

Amy Lowell's invitation to speak to Heterodoxy.

She dealt very pleasantly with her theories of poetry and such general subjects and then asked if anyone would like her to read some of her poems. That produced a landslide of requests. Member after member demanded a special favorite, and each selection was more sentimental than the last, which had dripped with sweet sorrows of one sort or another. It was all so sad that Rose Pastor Stokes turned around and laid her head on her neighbor's shoulder and cried down her neck, sobbing an obligato to Miss Lowell's sonorous voice. The poetess stood it as long as she could and then:

"I'm through," she said. "They told me I was to be speaking to a group of intellectual, tough-minded leaders in the women's world. Instead I find a group that wants nothing but my most sentimental things. Good afternoon!" And she poked her cigar into her mouth and walked out glowering.[14]

I can just see "Jo" Baker sitting there in her high-necked collar and tie, her finely tailored suit, and her close cropped hair, enjoying the equally tailored Amy Lowell's outburst. Those two closeted Lesbians had a lot in common, as Dr. Baker undoubtedly knew, including a fine disdain for "feminine" displays of tearful emotion.

Dr. Sara Josephine Baker

22

The very human quality of the few descriptions of Heterodoxy meetings make me eager to know more. These were flesh-and-blood women, not cardboard historical figures. Sometimes it is hard to believe that their meetings occurred seventy years ago, with the members wearing floor-length dresses instead of jeans. Yet almost all of the Heterodites were born in the nineteenth century, subject to the rigid social mores and code of their era. To get to Heterodoxy meetings, they had to fight a lot more than New York City traffic. All their lives, they fought the voices of conventional behavior. And some members fought their hardest battles against their internal dread of being seen as foolish or too "different."

Most Heterodites relished their differences, however. The member who sobbed so loudly during Amy Lowell's poetry reading was a young immigrant cigar maker who had recently married a socialist who also happened to be a millionaire. Rose Pastor Stokes was now a labor organizer, and had long been involved in socialist, suffrage, and labor causes. The member who described her sobs and Lowell's outburst was a middle-aged Lesbian doctor who was also the head of a large Bureau of the New York Public Health Department.

The American government certainly considered Heterodoxy's members worthy of more than casual interest. Before long, the entire group would be followed to meetings by government agents, some of the women would be accused of spying and being traitors to the United States, and founder Marie Jenney Howe would be arrested in front of her apartment building. Several other Heterodoxy members would be beaten in front of the White House, imprisoned for daring to question President Woodrow Wilson's anti-suffrage policies, and force-fed, brutally manhandled by prison guards, and psychologically tortured for daring to silently hold banners proclaiming women's right to vote.

It is sometimes hard to recall how much courage and conviction women of previous eras had to have to accomplish even the simplest political action. Our collective memory of these events is successfully dimmed even further by the textbooks and history lessons fed us since childhood, which more often than not patronize the minimal amount of women's history they pass on to us.[15] Women's political history, particularly the movement for the vote which takes so much of the little space devoted to women in high-school textbooks, would seem to be the most accessible, yet it is usually the most distorted. Difficult as it is to read some of the documents referred to in the following chapter, we must read if we are to understand anything at all of the possiblities inherent in us individually and collectively, as well as to understand the possible reactions that can and have been taken against us by the country we live in. We need to take an active interest in rediscovering and reevaluating our political heritage for a truer view of ourselves as women and as citizens.

Footnotes to Chapter 2

1. Ida Proper, "Heterodoxy to Marie" club album.
2. Beradine Kielty Scherman, *Girl From Fitchburg* (New York: Random House, 1964), p. 64.
3. I deeply appreciate the information provided by Patricia McC. Miller, and look forward with great interest to her forthcoming biography of Helen Hull.
4. Inez Haynes Irwin, "Adventures of Yesterday," unpublished autobiography in the Inez Haynes Irwin Papers, Arthur and Elizabeth Schlesinger Library, pp. 413-414.
5. Caroline Singer, noted as "Purloined from Cheng Kung Sui, died A.D. 273," "Heterodoxy to Marie" club album.
6. Mary Chamberlain, "Heterodoxy to Marie" club album.
7. Frances Maule, "Heterodoxy to Marie" club album.
8. Alice Duer Miller, "Heterodoxy to Marie" club album.
9. Inez Haynes Irwin, "Adventures," p. 414.
10. Ibid., p. 414.
11. Ibid., p. 422.
12. Heywood Hale Broun, *Whose Little Boy Are You?* (New York: St. Martin's, 1983), pp. 106-107.
13. Katharine Anthony to Ethel Sturges Dummer, October 1919, Ethel Sturges Dummer Papers.
14. Sara Josephine Baker, *Fighting for Life* (New York: Macmillan, 1939), pp. 182-183.
15. For example, see Karen M. Harbeck's excellent analysis of textbooks, "Remember the Ladies: The Presentation of Women in College-Level American History Textbooks" (Master's Thesis, San Jose State University, 1980).

Cooper Union and the Bowery, New York

Heterodoxy and Politics

To me feminism means that woman wants to develop her own womanhood. It means that she wants to push on to the finest, fullest, freest expression of herself. She wants to be an individual ...The freeing of the individuality of woman does not mean original sin; it means the finding of her own soul.[1]

So said Rose Young, the novelist, in 1914. She spoke for virtually all of Heterodoxy. Feminism was the one belief that united every member. Many of them were ardent workers for the cause of woman suffrage, but most did not let their feminism stop there. Still, the right to vote was seen as a valuable tool. Nearly all the members were at one time or another workers and marchers for the National American Woman Suffrage Association. Mary Ware Dennet was secretary of the NAWSA chapter in New York City from 1910 to 1915, while Bessie Beatty campaigned as a child with her mother in California in the 1890s. Dr. Sara Josephine Baker found herself "drawn," as she put it, "by 'psychological suction' into the woman suffrage movement."[2] The head of the Bureau of Child Hygiene, New York Health Department, Dr. Baker was one of the original members of the College Women's Equal Suffrage League. She could be counted on to give speeches to noon-hour Wall Street crowds of bemused and sometimes hostile men, as well as march in the annual suffrage parades along Fifth Avenue. Looking back on the 1910s, she felt that "we women had never had any position of importance in the world and . . . we had everything to gain."[3]

Some members had to face strong objections of their family and friends when they joined the suffrage movement. Zona Gale's mother viewed with great disfavor her daughter's activities on behalf of suffrage and other reform movements. "I would let that mess of women *alone*," she wrote her daughter.[4] Zona Gale did not listen. Similar pleas from other parents and husbands only made women more dedicated than ever to winning the vote. Mary Ware Dennett's divorce in 1913 was a direct result of her work as secretary of the NAWSA, since her husband "did not share these new interests."[5]

These women were strong fighters for the suffrage cause. The young women who entered the movement after the turn of the century believed that the time for victory was long overdue. They were dissatisfied with the same old tactics of private fund-raisers in homes, and the continual round of tired speakers saying the same old things at listless suffrage gatherings. In New York, an alternative could be found in the upstart organization, the Equality League of Self-Supporting Women (later renamed the Women's Political Union), founded in 1907 by Elizabeth Cady Stanton's daughter, Harriot Stanton Blatch. After being exposed to the militant suffrage tactics in England for several years, Blatch returned to America and found "the suffrage movement was

Suffragette's March

completely in a rut. . . . It bored its adherents and repelled its opponents."[6] She and her followers soon began to revive the New York movement, and by 1910 discovered one of the most successful devices for gaining public attention: the suffrage parades which became annual events in New York City.[7]

About this same time, Marie Jenney Howe arrived in New York and "threw herself into the suffrage movement" there as she had done in Cleveland. Organizing the Twenty-Fifth District of the New York City Woman Suffrage Party, she soon "gathered around her a brilliant group of workers."[8] One of them, Ida Proper was a future Heterodoxy member and artist who captained the Seventeenth Election Precinct in Howe's district.[9] Marie Howe was "a very effective suffrage organizer" who organized the district "in which she lived more completely than any Tammany district leader ever did."[10]

> Mrs. Howe seemed to me . . . to be curiously significant of the feminist movement of that time. . . . that religious instinct which led her first to the Church accompanied her always unconsciously in her suffrage and feminist activities; into these she carried the same religious fervor. Perhaps there were other women in Heterodoxy who went further along the passionate path of femininity than Marie Howe, but none of them had so much personal power and organizing ability. She was singularly devoted to all her friends in the cause of suffrage and to a deep-seated idealist feeling of the need of deep human relations.[11]

I'm not sure that "religious fervor" deserves all the credit, but Marie Howe did become one of the best political strategists in the New York suffrage movement. Her husband had become director of Greenwich Village People's Institute, "a kind of popular university, which conducted a public forum at Cooper Union" in the Village.[12] The public forum concept seemed to Marie Howe to be ready-made for the feminist cause, but she was determined not to hold the usual boring suffrage gathering of the past. What may have been the first group effort by Heterodoxy was held soon after the formation of the club in 1912. A forum called "Twenty-five Answers to Antis" was held at the Metropolitan Temple in New York. Most of the speakers were charter members of Heterodoxy. Fola La Follette's husband, playwright George Middleton, called it a "really exciting gathering" whose "sheer audacity sprang from the fertile brain of Marie Jenny Howe, who was also the Chairwoman: a most efficient one."

> Each speaker took a trite objection to suffrage and had five minutes
> to mop it up. Thirty seconds before the end of the alloted time
> Marie rang a bell. On the sentence her gavel would drop.[13]

No longer would audiences have to put up with the same long-winded speaker meandering on and on about women's right to vote. Marie Howe's dramatic solution gave the public twenty-five speakers, many of them well-qualified from their years on stage or lecture platform. Suspense was provided by the five-minute rule being rigorously carried out. Each speaker also had a definite, limited topic to answer; the more asinine the anti-suffrage argument each speech answered, the more colorful the reply.

The tactic proved a brilliant publicity ploy. Still, not every suffrage leader was happy with this innovation or approved of Heterodoxy's broader definition of feminism. As Fola LaFollette's husband, George Middleton, recalled:

> It seems rather strange that this whole feminist front should have
> aroused such intense feeling. . . . The old leaders, who had gallant-
> ly gone down the line exclusively for suffrage, and had long been its
> shock troops, were scared of the newer and more skittish recruits;
> for these were vocatively not after the vote alone, and were slash-
> ing . . . at every sex discrimination. . . . This was feminism in the
> real sense, suffrage being merely its political face.[14]

Two years later, in 1914, Marie Jenney Howe organized the two famous "feminist mass meetings" at Cooper Union under the title "What is Feminism?" Heterodoxy had moved on from suffrage speeches to addressing an entire spectrum of feminist issues. The *New York Times* coverage of both meetings was extensive, considering their usual minimal reporting of feminist news. Marie Howe was as good a diplomat as she was an organizer, and wrote the paper a thank-you letter "for myself, and for a large number of women who stand with me." She added: "I am told that *The Times* is an anti paper. If this is true, you deserve all the more credit for giving a square deal to our side."[15]

The first of the two Cooper Union meetings was held on February 17, 1914. The speeches were limited to ten minutes each. Admission was free, and the audience contained more men than women with the large auditorium filled to capacity. Floyd Dell, George Middleton, Max Eastman, and Will Irwin joined Frances Perkins, Jesse Lynch Williams, and Heterodoxy members Rose Young, Crystal Eastman, Henrietta Rodman, and Marie Howe (as chair) in speaking on the subject "What

WHAT IS FEMINISM?
COME AND FIND OUT

FIRST FEMINIST MASS MEETING

at the PEOPLE'S INSTITUTE, Cooper Union

Tuesday Evening, February 17th, 1914, at 8 o'clock, P. M.

Subject: "WHAT FEMINISM MEANS TO ME."

Ten-Minute Speeches by

ROSE YOUNG	GEORGE CREEL
JESSE LYNCH WILLIAMS	MRS. FRANK COTHREN
HENRIETTA RODMAN	FLOYD DELL
GEORGE MIDDLETON	CRYSTAL EASTMAN BENEDICT
FRANCES PERKINS	EDWIN BJORKMAN
WILL IRWIN	MAX EASTMAN

Chairman, MARIE JENNEY HOWE.

SECOND FEMINIST MASS MEETING

at the PEOPLES' INSTITUTE, Cooper Union

Friday, February 20th, 1914, at 8 o'clock, P. M.

Subject: "BREAKING INTO THE HUMAN RACE."

The Right to Work.—
RHETA CHILDE DORR

The Right of the Mother to Her Profession.—
BEATRICE FORBES-ROBERTSON-HALE.

The Right to Her Convictions.—
MARY SHAW.

The Right to Her Name.—
FOLA LA FOLLETTE.

The Right to Organize.—
ROSE SCHNEIDERMAN.

The Right to Ignore Fashion.—
NINA WILCOX PUTNAM.

The Right to Specialize in Home Industries.—
CHARLOTTE PERKINS GILMAN.

Chairman, MARIE JENNEY HOWE.

ADMISSION FREE.   *NO COLLECTION.*

Feminism Means to Me." *The New York Times* reported that:

> Marie Jenney Howe . . . said that feminism was "the entire woman movement," and she added that while men were held in a prison by convention, custom, and tradition, women were confined to one room in the prison and had to "watch the men walk about in the corridors in comparative freedom."[16]

The rights that women needed to have for "Breaking into the Human Race" was the topic of the second meeting, held three days later on February 20, 1914. Six feminists spoke, all of them members of Heterodoxy except for the trade unionist, Rose Schneiderman, who spoke on "The Right to Organize." The other speakers and subjects were: Rheta Childe Dorr, "The Right To Work"; Beatrice Forbes-Robertson Hale, "The Right of the Mother to Her Profession"; Mary Shaw, "The Right to Her Convictions"; Fola La Follette, "The Right to Her Name" (La Follette had kept her name after marriage); Nina Wilcox Putnam (inventor of a one-piece dress), "The Right to Ignore Fashion"; and Charlotte Perkins Gilman, on "The Right to Specialize in Home Industries."[17] At this meeting, Howe repeated her main concern: "We're sick of being specialized to sex," she cried. "We intend simply to be ourselves, not just our little female selves, but our whole, big, human selves."[18] This was a theme Marie Jenney Howe returned to often: the right of women to be "whole, big, human selves," not satisfied with the cardboard-cutout "feminine" role that men expected and wanted women to live down to. She felt that anything that stunted the growth of women was an abomination.

Fola La Follette

Elizabeth Gurley Flynn

Heterodoxy women involved in working and fighting for equal suffrage were also committed to many other liberal and radical issues. "I have no recollection of the term 'united front,'" Elizabeth Gurley Flynn wrote in her autobiography. The term was used much later by "red-baiting" conservatives to imply that almost all liberal groups were tied together in a great anti-American conspiracy directed by Communists according to instructions handed down from Moscow. But before the Russian Revolution in 1917, liberal-minded Americans joined causes with an ease that ignored political divisions and focused on needed reforms. As Elizabeth Gurley Flynn wrote in 1964, the term "united front"

> came into use much later. But to the extent to which the radical and progressive movements operated then on such a principle is very apparent. Men and women who spoke out for suffrage would also sign appeals for financial aid to the IWW and appear on Irish and amnesty delegations and were in the peace movement. There were no hard and fast lines drawn between one good freedom cause and another and no such fears of reprisal as there are today. People were not afraid they would hurt one cause by identifying themselves with another. I marvel today at how wide and diffuse were my contacts and friendships in those days.[19]

As member Mary Heaton Vorse recalled much later in an oral history interview:

> It was in the air. It was the time of Hull House. It was the time of social change. It was a natural thing. It was a time when great quantities of our people joined with the Socialist Party. . . . Rose Strunsky, a Heterodoxy member, had a lot of dynamite in her room, that she'd cached for someone. The owner of the house would come in and say 'I smell something stuffy in here.'
>
> Being social minded,—you didn't have to search at all, as you might today, because it was in the air. It was natural. . . . [20]

Many times, Heterodoxy members' experience in one political arena spilled over into other members' lives, helping to radicalize more than one Heterodite. Fola La Folette, who was at that time a Greenwich Village actress (and daughter of Senator Robert La Follette), was asked by the Women's Trade Union League to read some poetry to striking pickets during the "White Goods Workers' Strike."

> As she stood before them, she suddenly felt poetry was not enough for hungry eyes.
>
> "I only wish there was something I could *do*," she said, as she stopped
>
> A girl in back called out: "There is, Miss La Follette. You can go with us on the picket line. If there's a lady with us the police won't beat us up." Then she poured out how they had been "beaten up" by strikebreakers, hired "to break up the line."
>
> So Fola joined them. On the picket line she saw the brutal handling repeated upon another girl. When Fola protested the plain-clothes deputy showed his badge and carted the girl off to the Police Court. She was released to appear for trial that night, and Fola brought her to our flat. . . .
>
> We went that night to court. Fola testified as to what had happened, and was supported by (Heterodoxy member) Edna Kenton, the novelist, . . . But the Magistrate, who had an antilabor record, took the unsupported word of the detective. . . . The girl said to Fola afterwards: "I didn't do anything, and I got sentenced. I wish I had done something."[21]

Soon the pickets were joined by other middle-class and upper-class women, dismayed by Fola La Follette's well-publicized account of what was actually happening to the strikers. She made sure Jewish strikers were fed kosher sandwiches, went to the strikers' trials again and again, and was credited with making such a stirring speech about the strikers' need for money to pay the rent on their rooms that one man in the audience, with tears in his eyes, rounded up a thousand dollars overnight to pay the landlords so that the strike could continue.

Fola La Follette was raised, literally, in the Progressive movement which her father led for so long, and had honed her speaking skills on campaign platforms all over the country.

> The women's rights movement became one of that host of reform efforts falling under the rubric of Progressivism in the early twentieth century. The majority of women involved were "social feminists" who put social reform ahead of purely feminine issues. The inequities facing women made many of them sympathetic to demands for social reform generally; . . . Hence, they strongly sup-

ported prohibition, pure food and drugs, control and prevention of disease, elimination of prostitution and the double standard, creation of juvenile courts and reformatories for children, child labor laws, and compulsory school attendance.[22]

While many Heterodoxy members worked for some of the above reforms, few of them "put social reform ahead" of feminist issues. If some did, it was because they realized that some of those issues affected women's lives so deeply that they were, in fact, feminist issues.

Marie Jenney Howe and Fola La Follette were only two of many Heterodoxy women actively working for progressive reform, and their ties to other social issues brought in several new members throughout the 1910s and early 1920s. Heterodoxy members of the Women's Trade Union League included Katharine Anthony, stage manager Helen Arthur, Henrietta Rodman, Florence Woolston Seabury, and Rose Young. Grace Nail Johnson, the only Black woman who joined Heterodoxy, worked with her husband James Weldon Johnson in the civil rights work of the National Association for the Advancement of Colored People (NAACP). Interior decorator and artist Ami Mali Hicks was a member of not only the Trade Union League, but also the Women's Henry George League and the Manhattan Single Tax Club. She was joined in her advocacy of a single tax on land values by Mary Ware Dennett and Anna George de Mille. Agnes de Mille wrote about her mother that

> Before all else, Mother was the adoring disciple of her father, Henry George, and Single-Taxers the world over constituted a kind of second family. . . . Wherever we went thereafter, we were met by men and women who had corresponded for years with my mother and who opened their houses and hearts, even in Paris. . . .[23]

Henry George's philosophy of a single tax levied against the value of land would have eliminated all other taxes upon income, personal property, industry, buildings and improvements of buildings—in other words, only the landowners would have to pay taxes. This type of tax appealed to many progressive reformers, who viewed America's land as a resource which should be used for the welfare and benefit of all the people, not simply the ones who could afford to buy it.

"The progressive movement never really existed as a recognizable organization with common goals and a political machinery . . . to achieve them."[24] The closest the movement ever came to that was as a liberal faction of the Republican Party. Its strongest moment came in Senator Robert La Follette's thwarted bid for nomination as a presidential candidate in the 1912 election. Much later, when La Follette again ran for President in the 1924 election as an independent candidate, the progressive movement was already a political shambles, an idea whose time had passed in a new era of cynicism and profit-making. Heterodoxy members were forced to choose national political leaders from one of the two major parties or bolt the political system for the radical left of socialism and communism. Of course, many Heterodoxy women had joined the more radical left long before the twenties, especially those who lived in Greenwich Village. During the 1910's, Greenwich Village

Vira Whitehouse speaking on suffrage, Wall Street at noon
(from New York Tribune, 1913)

Suffrage parade, Washington D.C. 1913 (Library of Congress)

members were generally younger than other Heterodites, and often freer from social pressures and controls over their lives. Much of their freedom was a direct result of the new Bohemia in which they lived. A young Greenwich Village woman later recalled:

> New York's Bohemia before World War I was a spiritual haven. I doubt if ever in America there has been a spot where art and living, intertwined for a short time, brought forth such earnestness or such good companionship. It was a tiny island in the big city and its span of idyllic life was short—1912 to 1915. By 1916 it was already becoming self-conscious . . . .
> We were young and free, and our values were singularly true. Life in Bohemia was serious, and its ethical standards were probably higher than in most of the parts from which we had come.[25]

Villagers used the physical isolation of the Village to their advantage before the opening of the West Side subway in 1917. It became a sort of liberal/radical small town. The low rents attracted artists, writers, teachers and others who found that they would have the benefits of community camaradarie, with the urban advantage of few moral restrictions placed on their behavior. Villagers demanded ethical ideals, not traditional moral standards. The newcomers seldom mixed socially with the ethnic families of the Village. They were a community unto themselves, eating their meals at Polly Halliday's, then dropping by the offices of *The Masses* with their latest poem, drawing for the cover, cartoon, or article on feminism, Socialism, or the Industrial Workers of the World (IWW). In the evenings, Villagers enjoyed the free and abundant hospitality at the salon of the wealthy Heterodoxy member Mabel Dodge, where they might meet almost anyone active in anarchist, labor, socialist, and newspaper circles. Artists, actors, slumming social types from "uptown," writers, and politicians of every persuasion mingled at Mabel Dodge's during the heyday of the prewar Village.[26] Greenwich Village's other major evening social spot could be found at the Liberal Club. Henrietta Rodman and other members had split away from the original Liberal Club in Gramercy Square in the fall of 1913 over the older faction's refusal to admit Black members to the club. The anti-racist members moved to Macdougal Street above Polly Halliday's restaurant, where they occupied three sparsely furnished, high ceilinged rooms. Despite the many references to the Liberal Club in autobiographies of pre-war Village radicals, it was never more than "primarily a social meeting place," although it did serve

> as a focal point where all the young men and women who were interested in what was new in the arts and economics mixed and mutually stimulated one another.[27]

Socialism was the prevailing political belief among liberal and radical Villagers before World War I.

> No other political party or organization embodied the social values of the various women's rights organizations as did the Socialist Party; no other group fought as consistently for the full enfranchisement of women. In return, women flocked into the Party, playing an active role in its affairs on many levels of the organiza-

34

Henrietta Rodman

tion, from the lowest to the highest. In this respect, the Socialist Party is unique among American parties, past and present.[28]

Village suffragists "saw feminism as the value system that would accompany the new socialist order." Heterodoxy Socialists Susan Glaspell, Henrietta Rodman, Rose Pastor Stokes, Rheta Childe Dorr, Lou Rogers, Florence Woolston Seabury, Ida Rauh and Crystal Eastman

faithfully believed in the eventual transformation of the United States into a cooperative commonwealth. It was only a matter of time. Ida Rauh wagered a young friend of hers in 1912 that within ten years the United States would be a socialist republic. After seeing the bleak realities of industrialism in the neighborhood slums, Villagers were convinced that American workers would not, and could not, tolerate their deplorable working conditions much longer.[29]

The naivete of the Village Socialists was matched by their vigorous energy on behalf of these goals. The most articulate outlet for the Village philosophy was the radical publication, *The Masses*, which Max Eastman, Crystal's brother, edited. An always enthusiastic, often humorous, and certainly inspiring voice for all that was vital in Village political thinking, *The Masses* became an internationally famous periodical while still remaining a Village enterprise and an organ for the neighborhood's prevailing interests. Max Eastman wrote that *The Masses*

. . . provided for the first time in America, a meeting ground for revolutionary labor and the radical intelligentsia. It acquired, in spite of its gay laughter, the character of a crusade.[30]

Many Heterodoxy members read and contributed to the pro-feminist *Masses*, especially Elsie Clews Parsons, Mary Heaton Vorse, Marie Jenney Howe, and Inez Haynes Irwin.

The strength of the Village feminists has often been commented on, particularly by the historian June Sochen. However, we are seldom told how many of those feminists were also lesbians. Then, as now, the Village had a reputation as a "safe haven" for lesbians and homosexual men. Most of Heterodoxy's lesbian members preferred to live in the Village, as much for its low rents as for its welcome laissez-faire attitude towards those who dared to deviate from standard heterosexuality. Katharine Anthony and Elisabeth Irwin, Frances Maule, Kathleen de Vere Taylor and several other probable lesbians rented Village flats. They lived urban, women-centered lives, which allowed them to ignore the sort of social pressures that family-centered and small-town lesbians had to face. It was too early for lesbian and gay political activism; no formal or even informal organizational structure had yet evolved in America for lesbians or gay men. Their political identity, as far as I can tell, seems to have come less from their lesbianism than from their feminism, although they did hotly debate Freud's sexual theories. During at least the first decade of Heterodoxy's existence, women couples often were acknowledged on the same par as male-female couples. Anniversary dates were recognized and the lesbian couples received strong emotional support from most Heterodites when one of the partners was sick or died. Outside of Heterodoxy, the lesbians were politically involved in the same sort of issues as other members.

However, within the club, members were not always of one mind about lesbianism, or even about the issue of whether a feminist should feel free to stay single and/or childless. After the first edition of this book came out, historian Nancy Cott informed me of an exchange of letters between Heterodoxy member Ruth Pickering and her sister-in-law, Mrs. C. B. Pinchot, regarding Helen Hull.

Author Helen Hull wrote over sixty short stories and twenty-five novels during her lifetime, including one short story and two novels cited by pioneer lesbian scholar Jeannette Foster in *Sex Variant Women in Literature*[31]: "The Fire," published in *Century Magazine* in 1919, *Quest* (1922), and *The Labyrinth* (1923). In each, she wrote of what she knew from first hand experience—women loving women, and women in couples. Her writing was based in part upon her life with children's book author Mabel Louise Robinson, whom she had met when they were both instructors at Wellesley College in 1912. In their collected papers are glowing tributes to their fifty years of life together, including hand-made booklets of poetry, photographs tied with scarlet ribbon, and a hand-made paper doll of a very boyish Helen Hull in jodpurs. One booklet dated 1914 is from "A Knight to His Lady" (Helen Hull to Mabel Louise Robinson). That was the year they left the confines of Wellesley to become English instructors at Columbia University. They enjoyed their life together as a middle-class New York lesbian couple, spending the winters teaching, going to the theater, attending literary events and suffrage meetings as they developed a wide circle of friends. In the summer months, they sublet their apartment and retreated to their farm on the coast of Maine, where they wrote during the mornings and sailed away the afternoons, often in the company of other lesbian couples and friends.

Somehow in the first few years in New York, Helen Hull became a member of Heterodoxy. Mabel Louise Robinson apparently never joined the group (although she did attend some functions), nor did she become a member of the Authors Guild, the writers' organization where Helen devoted so much energy and time. Helen Hull's closest ties within Heterodoxy seem to have been with Katharine Anthony, Elisabeth Irwin (another lesbian couple who were instructors at Wellesley College during the same years as Hull and Robinson), Dr. Frances Maule and Mryan Louise Grant. Helen Hull began her writing career as one of the rare women authors who dared to touch the theme of women who loved women. *The Labyrinth* tells of a separate, very enjoyable world of single urban middle-class women with their own clubs, groups of friends, and social life.[32] But by the mid-1920s, Freud's penis-envy theories and other psychological/medical testimony calling lesbians "sick," "perverted," and "deviant" had filtered down into the popular magazines, newspapers, and public consciousness so thoroughly that as Heterodite playwright Susan Glaspell said, "You couldn't go out to buy a bun without hearing of someone's complex." Helen Hull stopped writing about healthy women couples, turning instead to tales of complex unhappy heterosexual relationships. Her writing gained in popularity and sales. An awareness of changing public attitudes towards any hint of lesbianism and her growing desire for privacy drove her publishers frantic as she refused many requests to submit to interviews and autograph sessions. Some of the more personal circumstances driving her into a more insular private world are not yet known.[33] However, one particular moment of pain was witnessed by Mrs. C. B. Pinchot, sister-in-law of Ruth Pinchot Pickering, and an invited guest at the January 9th, 1927 Heterodoxy meeting. As you read the following excerpts from her account of the meeting, note her ease and familiarity with 1920s popular psychology. Never having met Helen Hull before, she attempts to make sense of Helen's obvious horror in hearing respected friends and co-members state flatly that women who refused heterosexual marriage for any reason could not be considered as embodying the highest feminist values. Mrs. Pinchot wrote:

> I really did enjoy the Heterodoxites (sic) immensely yesterday, and I am so grateful to you for taking me. You don't know how exciting it was to hear (literally) those women's minds clash and function. After the stodgy silliness of the talkative Republican ladies and the complacent chatterings of the Harrisburg elite, it seemed wonderful and gay—and very much worth while.

She then added:

> One thing interested or rather bothered me terribly in that meeting. I wonder whether you noticed it—or whether it was all my imagination? It was the woman who sat two places to the left of Doctor Hollingworth. I think her name was Miss Hull. It seemed to me that something awfully cruel was done to her at that meeting—and I felt that she was going through hell all the time. I had a feeling that she had gone through a hell of a life when she was younger—realizing that she was starved emotionally—and that she

was lonely and becoming embittered—and then later on, perhaps a few years ago, she had built up through the modern psychological jargon a kind of protective philosophy for her own sublimination—and all the rest of it—which had brought her some kind of peace.

When Doctor Hollingworth included in her definition of perfect feminist a woman happily married and with children, it shattered all Miss Hull's defense mechanism. Did you notice how she turned to the other psychoanalyst with white hair (Doctor Potter, wasn't it?) and to one or two others, and hoped they would back her up—and when they did not, did you see her face and notice that she never spoke again?

I wonder whether you know anything about her? I may be a fool, but I think there was a good deal of tragedy for her involved in that situation. I don't see that there is anything to be done about it—but it seemed too pitiful to destroy someone's way of life —and it seemed to me that she was the kind of person who had made a philosophy out of words.

Ruth Pickering replied:

. . . Perhaps you were right about Helen Hull, but I didn't notice it. Helen Hull has written two successful novels and I gathered from what she said is about to publish another. I'll get the names of her books and send them to you. I don't know why but I was never drawn to her much—didn't know her well at all. . . . I thought in a round-about way, she was trying to get either Leta Hollingworth or Grace Potter to tell her that in creating literature she had fulfilled herself as well as if she had created a baby. Possibly this did show an unhappy doubt in her mind. But I don't think she learned anything new during that discussion; I should guess she was fairly well onto herself.[34]

Mabel Louise Robinson (left rear) and Helen Hull (right front) with friends in Maine, 1920's

Helen Hull's love letters to and from Mabel Louise Robinson, as well as the photographs from the 1910s and early 20s, show us not a sublimated, emotionally starved unhappy woman, but a proud, strong and sexually fulfilled lesbian. Whether she yearned for a child, I don't really know, but none of the many hundreds of documents I have seen refer to children at all. (I also think it is quite interesting that the statement was made by childless Leta Hollingworth, who found her own marriage very confining.) It is possible by the 1920s, Helen Hull had already begun her long battle with alcoholism, or that she'd simply been appalled to hear such backtracking statements which excluded so many women from feminism. But beyond Helen's personal distress, this exchange of letters tells us much of the changing ethics and ideals of feminism after women won the right to vote. By 1927, even within Heterodoxy's haven from unquestioned majority viewpoints, feminism had gone from the open-ended 1910's hope of sexual and economic freedom to the narrow limitations of hetero-sexual marriage and motherhood all over again. No lesbians need apply.

One of the strongest political battles Heterodoxy members were caught up in was labor's right to unionize for decent wages and working conditions. They invited the young radical activist Elizabeth Gurley Flynn to speak before the club. In 1915, Flynn had been arrested at a silk strike in Paterson, New Jersey, for her organizing activities. She was released on bail awaiting her trial, when according to her biography, she

> . . . was invited to speak on the IWW and its activities in the organization of women in the textile industry before a unique group in New York City. . . . called the "Heterodoxy." Marie Jenney Howe, whom I had met in Cleveland with Tom L. Johnson, was its chairman. It shunned publicity, but as its name implied had free and frank discussions on all subjects. I was invited to join after my speech.[35]

Heterodoxy was so enthralled by its new member that Fola La Folette, Margaret Wycherly, and other members joined reformers from many other New York groups in organizing a defense committee which paid for lawyers for Flynn's trial. Henrietta Rodman and others also demonstrated for Flynn's right to free speech when the organizer attempted to return to Paterson before the trial. Mabel Dodge gave a large sum of money to the Industrial Workers of the World to hire Madison Square Garden for one night in order to stage a huge IWW labor pageant, a theatre of the people that had never been seen before. Flynn was acquitted, and for the first time found herself enjoying the "broadening influence" in getting to "know all those splendid Heterodoxy members. . . . It made me conscious of women and their many accomplishments."[36]

By the time Flynn joined Heterodoxy, many of the club members, including Marie Jenney Howe, had left the National Woman Suffrage Association for its more militant counterpart, the Congressional Union. In 1916, that organization's name was changed to the National Woman's

Party, and most of the members' political activity revolved around either the NWP or the Women's Peace Party.

With the ever-increasing involvement of the United States in the war which had been raging throughout Europe since 1914, pacifism became *the* decisive issue in Heterodoxy. The club was split over the question of pacifism versus involvement in war preparation as they had never been over any other issue. One of the first members to resign from the club was the journalist, Rheta Childe Dorr. "The outbreak of World War I radically altered Mrs. Dorr's views, drawing her away from her earlier reformist causes and friends."[37] She left Heterodoxy, saying "alternate Saturday lunches had no more attractions for me."[38] In reality, of course, it was the conversation at those luncheons that no longer attracted her, since so many Heterodoxy members were strong and vocal pacifists. Charlotte Perkins Gilman soon followed Dorr, although she renewed her personal connections with Marie Jennie Howe and other Heterodoxy members during the 1920s.

When Senator La Follette became one of only six members of Congress to vote against the United States' entrance into the First World War, the harassment of pacifists in America began. Members of Heterodoxy, pacifists and patriotic war supporters alike, found themselves under surveillance. Dr. Baker reported:

> Yes, odd events happened in those queerly kinetic years. I had the privilege, shared with a great many other women, of being suspected of mildly radical sympathies which during the war were, of course, synonymous with giving aid and comfort to the enemy. I was no pacifist whatever. . . . But I did belong to a luncheon club for women active in various social and economic movements, and that was apparently enough. The name of the club was . . . Heterodoxy. Perhaps it was the name that alarmed the spy-chasers. Perhaps it was true, as legend said, that a worried member of Heterodoxy had written a letter calling on the secret service men to keep an eye on the club's weekly meetings because its rolls contained so many pacifists and radicals. The fantastic result was that we really did have to shift our meeting-place every week to keep from being watched. It was just like an E. Phillips Oppenheim novel. All except the characters, that is. My colleagues in treason were not sloe-eyed countesses with small pearl-handled revolvers in their pocketbooks, but people like Crystal Eastman, Fannie Hurst, Rose Pastor Stokes, Inez Haynes Irwin, Fola La Follette, and Mabel Dodge Luhan.[39]

To secret service agents, Rose Pastor Stokes would have been an even better catch than a "countess with a pearl-handled revolver." The petite ex-cigar maker who married millionaire socialist J. G. Phelps Stokes, had left the Socialist Party with her husband when the United States entered the war in April 1917. But after the successful Russian Revolution in November of the same year, she returned to making ardent speeches for the socialists, more committed than ever to their goals. In March 1918, she wrote a letter correcting a *Kansas City Star* account of one of her speeches, in which she declared: "I am for the

Rose Pastor Stokes

people, while the Government is for the profiteers." For that letter, Stokes was sentenced under the infamous and all-encompassing Espionage Act to ten years imprisonment. Although the sentence was overturned in 1920 by a court of appeals, Stokes had lost what little faith she had ever had in American democratic government, and by 1919 she had left socialism for the newly formed American Communist Party.[40]

Elizabeth Gurley Flynn recalled:

> After war was declared a mounting wave of hysteria and mob violence swept the country. It was not shared by the majority of American people who became increasingly intimidated. Printed signs were tacked up in public places: "Obey the law and keep your mouth shut!" signed by Attorney General Gregory. The victims were varied. . . .[41]

On September 29, 1917, Elizabeth Gurley Flynn was the only woman arrested in the Chicago mass indictment of 168 persons. The charge against them was vague in the extreme: "conspiracy to hinder and delay the execution of certain laws of the United States."

> Our next problem was to raise a defense fund to pay our lawyers and our fares to Chicago when we were called there for arraignment. We were all very poor. There was no type of defense organization then in existence. A group of women organized a special committee for me, and we also set up a general defense fund for ourselves. We raised and spent about $5,000. I recall a conversation I had the first day I was out on bail with Fola La Folette . . . who said: "I have no money for bail. But here's a little for your expenses." She never knew, I am sure, how much I appreciated that $5.00![42]

Whether the "group of women" who set up the special committee for Flynn was composed mostly of Heterodoxy women, I don't know. It is certainly possible. She later could remember "only one unpleasant experience" during the many years she belonged to Heterodoxy. It was an event which occurred during the war. She recalled "a few super-patriots were shocked at the anti-war sentiments freely expressed at our meetings. They demanded the expulsion of Rose Pastor Stokes and myself after we had been arrested. When the club refused, they re-signed."[43]

It is difficult to know exactly who the departing "super-patriots" were, other than that Rheta Childe Dorr and Charlote Perkins Gilman were among them. George Middleton wrote that he and Fola La Follette were good friends with Charlotte Perkins Gilman "until the war separated us. Charlotte had little tolerance for those who opposed our entrance into it."[44] Dorr eventually became a conservative in the Republican Party, a far cry from her early Socialist Party days. Gilman did contribute her photo and poem to the 1920 gift album, possibly out of

Rheta Childe Dorr
ready for war

(newspaper clipping)

respect to Marie Jenney Howe, whom she still admired. Stokes and Flynn remained in Heterodoxy, where there was "the strongest taboo on taboo," as Florence Woolston Seabury put it in her spoof of club customs.

> Heterodites say that taboo is injurious to free development of the mind and spirit. . . . By preventing taboo the tribe has been able to preserve considerable unanimity of variety in opinion.[45]

Few other organizations during World War I would have allowed such "un-American" sentiments as Stokes, Flynn and other pacifist members of Heterodoxy expressed during the war. In the overriding patriotic mentality, Heterodoxy meetings became a welcome refuge for some of the more persecuted members. Even within their own homes, Heterodoxy members like Elsie Clews Parsons fought a lonely battle against wartime jingoism. When her husband deliberately sought out an Army commission in August, 1917, he wrote from Washington "Today I received my orders for active duty & I suppose I am due in uniform tomorrow. No longer am I master of myself." Elsie wrote back: "Today I pity you, tomorrow you enrage, intellectually one loses interest, & that's the devil."[46] For the next year, she refused to allow anyone wearing a uniform to enter her home, including her husband. Herbert Parsons had been a U.S. Representative from New York in 1905-1911 and an Executive Committee member of the Republican National Committee. His letters home from overseas show a masculine view of the war strikingly different from that held by most of Heterodoxy, and certainly by Elsie Clews Parsons. In August, 1918, he wrote:

> William James was all wrong when he argued that there were moral substitutes for war. However hard it is, nothing brings to so many men such excitement & always on the border of danger. I am reminded of what the young French aviator in Washington last summer told me, that it was the greatest game in the world. This does not mean that our people want a world of war. I have nowhere heard such an idea. . . .I have been having a grand time.[47]

The "greatest game in the world?" It is no wonder that so many women joined with Mary Ware Dennett in the Women's Peace Party and Crystal Eastman in the American Union Against Militarism. The political propaganda machine drove home the view that any sort of anti-war sentiment was tantamount to treason.

Fola La Follette had to withstand intense public abuse over her father's, Senator Robert La Follette, vote against the war and his much-publicized speech in September, 1917.

> In a thousand newspapers across the country headlines quoted La Follette as having said that America had "no" grievances against Germany, when, in fact, he had shouted, "I don't mean to say that we hadn't suffered grievances; we had—at the hands of Germany. Serious grievances!" Heterodoxy member Zona Gale, herself a pacifist, was shocked by the lamentable aftermath. Immediately La Follette was attacked from all sides. Newspapers screamed his disloyalty.[48]

In the following months before her father finally proved that he had been misquoted, Heterodoxy meetings became one of the few places Fola La Follette could go to where "no one . . . paid any attention to war hysterias. Fola was Fola, as she had always been." On the streets, Mabel Dodge Luhan reported:

> People snubbed her, cut her, and behaved like idiot barbarians. She ceased to go about much but she generally came to Heterodoxy luncheons. That was a safe refuge. Everybody was glad to see her, . . . She would come in looking somewhat pale and pinched, but after an hour in that warm fellowship her face flushed and her muscles relaxed. It must have been a comfort to come there.[49]

Once again, Heterodoxy aided a member through a crisis. The club members could consistently be counted on to give shelter, loans, strong support, political alliance, and a shoulder to cry on when needed, as well as their collective voices to cry out against political injustice. That apt 1960's women's liberation slogan, "The Personal is Political," would have been easily understood by these early feminists.

Many other women, both in and out of Heterodoxy, did find the war to be more of a blessing than a curse. However they felt about the bloodshed itself, the advantages for women in employment opportunities were highly prized.[50] For the first time, their energy, skills and time were not only wanted by their country, they were actually needed. It was an era of opportunity for women, and they answered the call for war workers, nurses, Red Cross volunteers, and replacements for newly enlisted male employees in ever increasing numbers. The war even won for them the long-awaited vote. In January 1918, Woodrow Wilson finally endorsed the suffrage amendment, ending years of opposition, stating that "the war could not have been prosecuted without the women," and the best way America could repay its debt to them was by granting them equal suffrage. "He felt that women must participate in the post war reconstruction."[51]

This was after years of increasingly radical tactics brought to bear upon the government by the National Woman's Party which was led by Alice Paul. Inez Milholland had died of pernicious anemia at the end of 1916 after a heavy round of speaking commitments for the cause. Other women had been radicalized by their experiences on the picket lines the NWP set up around the White House beginning in January 1917. Pickets even circled the grounds on Woodrow Wilson's inauguration in March. By summer, though, the government tried to force pickets to give up their demonstrations by jailing them. In June 1917, the first group of picketing women were arrested and sentenced to jail terms. Eventually, four Heterodoxy members served jail sentences. Alison Turnbull Hopkins and Doris Stevens were arrested July 14, 1917, for picketing and sentenced to sixty days in the infamous Occoquan workhouse. Doris Stevens' descriptions of the treatment they received and the food they were served in the workhouse is enough to make a strong stomach sick. Woodrow Wilson, U.S. President at the time, made sure the jail officials knew that they should make the entire experience so unpleasant that other women would think twice before continuing the

Paula Jakobi

picketing and protest. But he wasn't prepared as yet to handle the
intense criticism and protest caused by influential husbands and other
male supporters of the jailed women. In three days, they were released,
pardoned by the President.

That was not the end of either the picketing or the arrests, however.
Paula Jakobi, a lesbian who had once worked as a matron at the Framingham (Massachusetts) women's prison so that she could study the
prison conditions, found herself on the other side of the bars after her
arrest on November 10, 1917. She and forty-five other suffragists were
sent to the Occoquan workhouse where they were roughly manhandled, threatened with being locked in the male prisoners' cells, with no
privacy from male eyes while urinating or defecating, and, finally,
forcibly held down and fed through tubes stuffed down their throats
when they refused to eat the disgusting, rotten food. Paula Jakobi
served thirty days there.[52]

Heterodite Alice Kimball, a New York librarian, was the last member
to be arrested, on August 10, 1918. She was among a group of suffragists
sentenced to fifteen days in the D.C. jail for simply taking part in a
meeting in Lafayette Square.

As the historian Eleanor Flexner makes clear, the suffrage pickets
were

> actually among the earliest victims of the abrogation of civil liber-
> ties in wartime. Most discussions of this issue confine themselves
> to the Government's actions under the Espionage Act, its treat-

ment of the I.W.W., Socialists . . . , and conscientious objectors. The fact remains that, once the suffrage arrests began, they were invariably confined to the pickets and never included the men who tore the banners from their hands and destroyed them, and often physically mistreated the women. While their slogans obviously were inflammatory, the women were never once arrested for disturbing the peace, inciting to riot, or jeopardizing the security of the country or its Chief Executive.

At first the pickets were dismissed without sentence. But as picketing and violence continued, the District courts began to sentence the women to jail, gradually increasing the term from a few days to six weeks and eventually to six months. A total of 218 women from 26 states were arrested. 97 went to prison. [53]

Still, it probably wasn't their heroic actions that finally won women the vote, as much as it was the role of women workers during the war, plus the "mounting crescendo of suffrage work under the leadership of the National Suffrage Association."[54] Even after the woman's suffrage amendment was passed and sent to the states for their approval in June 1919, there was a long and bitter struggle on the state level, but the battle for the vote was eventually victorious.

The First World War was over, too, but not the persecutions inflicted upon liberals and radicals under the Espionage Act, which had turned from war hysteria against pacifists and Germans into a device to be used against Communists, Socialists, and all others who deviated from "one-hundred per cent Americanism." *The Masses* was forced to cease publication in 1917: it had been revived in a slightly different form as *The Liberator* (1918-1921), but the old Greenwich Village group had scattered after the war, and the new publication never gained the enormous reputation that the defunct *Masses* had enjoyed. [55]

Frederic and Marie Jenney Howe were especially under attack during this period due to Fred Howe's position as the Commissioner of Immigration of the Port of New York, which he had held since 1914. He made an easy target for red-baiters and conservative patriots with his articulate public stand for due process before deportation of the thousands of "red sympathizers" rounded up under the Espionage Act. Howe wrote:

> I do not know why I suffered so much from this particular hysteria and the cruelties incident to it. . . . But I think it was the indignities suffered by friends that aroused me most. People came to me from all over the country. . . . All of them were seeking a refuge which could only be found in a government official. Few people know of the state of terror that prevailed during those years. . . . The prosecution was directed against liberals, radicals, persons who had been identified with municipal-ownership fights, with labor movements, with forums, with liberal papers which were under the ban. . . . I hated the Department of Justice, the ignorant secret-servicemen who had been intrusted [*sic.*] with man-hunting powers. . . . I hated the suggestion of disloyalty of myself and my friends. . . . [56]

On January 12, 1919, Senator Robert La Follette wrote to his wife, relating "an authentic but 'very ugly story' " he had recently heard in Washington concerning Marie Jenney Howe. "She had been seized in front of her apartment in New York by the 'Secret Service Hounds' and not allowed to communicate with her husband or an attorney."[57] How long she was held or why, his letter never said, nor does Frederic Howe refer to the incident in his autobiography. I have tried to verify this account through several sources, but still haven't been able to guarantee its authenticity. Still, it is probable that she was held for questioning for a short time, possibly about her husband's activities, or the activities of Heterodoxy members. Since Dr. Baker referred to Heterodoxy having to "shift our meeting place every week to keep from being watched," I find it easy to believe that someone in the government found the women troublesome enough to follow around and persecute. In my search of old microfilmed records at the National Archives, I came across evidence that other feminists, including Heterodite Crystal Eastman, were followed and spied upon, and that their landlords reported on their activities.[58] So, it is very probable that Marie Jenney Howe was arrested, exactly as La Follette told his wife.

Soon after this arrest, Marie Howe became ill with a heart condition, and retired from all her commitments except Heterodoxy meetings. She was now in her fifties, as were many of the early members of the club. She continued to chair the group for several more years until ill health forced her resignation.

The decade of the 1920s was a relatively quiet one for Heterodoxy members in the political sense. After winning the vote, they left the battlefield to the younger, more eager women in the social reform ranks, being content mainly to offer their writing talents, their names, and their money to the various causes that continued to spring up. Some of the women worked quietly on as volunteers for the League of Women Voters or for peace, but the only Heterodoxy members who continued to fight conspicuously for political change were the remaining Socialists, who were now moving into the Communist Party. Elizabeth Gurley Flynn, Rose Pastor Stokes, and Ruth Hale constantly appear in newspaper and historical accounts of the 1920s and 1930s. Hale was especially active during the Sacco-Vanzetti anarchist trial in Boston, being arrested in 1927 along with other prominent men and women picketing the courthouse in Boston for justice for the two Italian workers. Trips to Russia, books, articles, strikes, imprisonment, trials, appeals, and countless speeches and meetings occupied Stokes and Flynn until Stokes' death of cancer in 1933 and Flynn's in Russia in 1964.

Some Heterodoxy members came out of the First World War and its "Red Menace" aftermath with a bitter taste in their mouths about the ideals they had once believed in. Alice Rohe wrote in 1920: "Heterodoxy, to me, is an oasis in that great American desert—a world made safe for mediocrity."[59] Rohe's bitterness and anger with the turn of events in the America of the 1920s was all the stronger for the high ideals and hopes she had held for the United States before the war. Mediocrity was never highly prized by Heterodoxy women.

Younger members of Heterodoxy, like Anna George de Mille's daughter, Agnes de Mille, were more interested and excited about their flourishing careers than politics. Even the older members who had professions were enjoying the more advantageous climate for career women of the 1920s. Sara Josephine Baker recalled later:

> It seemed for a time—certainly after they received the right to vote—as though the way were clear and open before them. For several years women went constantly forward.[60]

Pickets arrested at the Capitol

(from *Jailed for Freedom* by Doris Stevens).

Footnotes to Chapter 3

1. "Talk on Feminism Stirs Great Crowd," *New York Times*, February 18, 1914, p. 2.
2. *Notable American Women: 1607-1950*, s.v. "Baker, Sara Josephine," by Leona Baumgartner.
3. Baker, p. 246.
4. Harold P. Simonson, *Zona Gale* (New York: Twayne Pub., 1962), p. 47.
5. *Notable American Women: 1607-1950*, s.v. "Dennett, Mary Ware," by Christopher Lasch.
6. Eleanor Flexner, *Century of Struggle* (New York, Atheneum, 1974), p. 250.
7. Ibid., p. 253.
8. Howe, p. 232.
9. *Women's Who's Who of America, 1914-1915*, s.v. "Proper, Ida Sedgwick."
10. Hapgood, p. 332.
11. Ibid., pp. 332-333.
12. Howe, p. 240.
13. George Middleton, *These Things Are Mine*, (New York: Macmillan, 1947), p. 125.
14. Ibid., p. 129-130.
15. Letter to *The New York Times*, February 27, 1914, p. 10.
16. *New York Times*, February 18, 1914, p. 2.
17. Middleton, p. 129.
18. "Feminist Meeting at Cooper Union," *The New York Times*, February 21, 1914, p. 18.
19. Elizabeth Gurley Flynn, *The Rebel Girl* (New York: International Publishers, 1973), p. 279.
20. Mary Heaton Vorse interviewed by Donald Shaughnessy, Columbia University Oral History Collection, 1957.
21. Middleton, pp. 115-116.
22. J. Stanley Lemons, "Social Feminism in the 1920s: Progressive Women and Industrial Legislation," *Labor History 14* (Winter 1973): 83.
23. Agnes de Mille, *Speak to Me, Dance With Me* (Boston: Little, Brown & Co., 1973), p. 70.
24. Arthur S. Link, "What Happened to the Progressive Movement in the 1920s?" in *Twentieth-Century America: Recent Interpretations*, ed. Barton J. Bernstein and Allen J. Matusow (New York: Harcourt, Brace & World, 1969), p. 118.
25. Scherman, p. 60.
26. Gilman M. Ostrander, *American Civilization in the First Machine Age: 1890-1940* (New York: Harper & Row, 1970), pp. 181-183.
27. Lawrence Langer, *The Magic Curtain* (New York: E.P. Dutton, 1951), pp. 72-73.
28. James Weinstein, *The Decline of Socialism in America, 1912-1925* (New York: Vintage, 1967), p. 54. For a fuller analysis, you will want to read Mari Jo Buhle's fascinating study, *Women and American Socialism, 1890-1920* (Chicago: University of Illinois Press, 1981).

29. June Sochen, *The New Woman in Greenwich Village, 1910-1920.* (New York: Quadrangle Books, 1972).
30. Ostrander, p. 180.
31. Jeannette H. Foster, *Sex Variant Women in Literature* (London: Frederick Muller Ltd, 1958).
32. As Jonathan Katz states in *Gay American History* (New York: Thomas Crowell, 1976), *"The Labyrinth* presents a rare picture of an aspiring, professionally employed Lesbian couple in the early 1920s. Hull's portrait of this couple is remarkable for its positive, matter-of-fact treatment, and for connecting this Lesbianism with an emphatic, though decidedly middle-class, feminism." *The Labyrinth* (New York: Macmillan, 1923).
33. Patricia McC. Miller's forthcoming study of Helen Hull's life and writings promises to help answer many of these questions.
34. C.B. Pinchot Collection, Box 105, Library of Congress. I deeply appreciate that so many interested women (and a few men) have been so generous in sharing information they have come across about Heterodoxy while pursuing their own scholarly interests. A particularly heartfelt "Thank You!" to Nancy Cott for this important reference, which would have been nearly impossible to discover on my own.
35. Flynn, p. 279.
36. Ibid., p. 280.
37. *Notable American Women: 1607-1950,* s.v. "Dorr, Rheta Childe," by Louis Filler.
38. Banner, p. 137.
39. Baker, p. 280.
40. *Notable American Women: 1607-1950,* s.v. "Stokes, Rose Pastor" by David A. Shannon.
41. Flynn, p. 229.
42. Ibid., p. 233.
43. Ibid.
44. Middleton, p. 280.
45. See "Marriage Customs and Taboo Among the Early Heterodites," Appendix B.
46. Peter H. Hare, *A Woman's Quest for Science: Portrait of Anthropologist Elsie Clews Parsons* (New York: Prometheus Books, 1985), p. 117.
47. Hare, pp. 119-120.
48. Simonson, p. 69.
49. Luhan, p. 144.
50. See the chapter on women and World War I in J. Stanley Lemon's *The Woman Citizen: Social Feminism in the 1920s* (Urbana, Ill.: University of Illinois Press, 1973), pp. 1-34.
51. Ibid., p. 13.
52. See Inez Haynes Irwin, *The Story of the Woman's Party* (New York: Harcourt, Brace & Co., 1921), and especially Doris Stevens' *Jailed for Freedom* (New York: Boni and Liveright, 1920), for one of the most stirring, anger-provoking books ever written about American radical feminist politics. This book has been republished by Schocken Books (New York: 1976).

53. Flexner, pp. 284-285.
54. Ibid., p. 287.
55. Stanley Cohen, "A Study in Nativism: The American Red Scare of 1919-1920," in *Twentieth-Century America: Recent Interpretations*, ed. Barton J. Bernstein and Allen J. Matusow (New York: Harcourt, Brace & World, 1969), pp. 88-109.
56. Howe, pp. 278-279.
57. La Follette, p. 2:938.
58. See Record Group 65, "Investigative Case Files of Bureau of Investigation, 1908-1924," Federal Bureau of Investigation Records, National Archives and Records Service.
59. Alice Rohe, "Heterodoxy to Marie" club album.
60. Baker, p. 246.

Banner carried in Suffrage parades, NYC. ©1915

Mary Knoblauch

Caroline Singer

"... Women Who Did Things ..."

As I look round and see your faces —
The actors, the editors, the businesswomen, the artists —
The writers, the dramatists, the psychoanalysts, the dancers
The doctors, the lawyers, the propagandists.
As I look round and see your faces
It really seems quite common to do anything!
Only she who does nothing is unusual.[1]

Paula Jakobi's inscription in the 1920 club album sums up Heterodoxy's general attitude towards women and work very well. As Inez Haynes Irwin noted, "Most of the women of Heterodoxy were through their own efforts economically independent."[2] In other words, they worked, and did not live off a husband's, father's or partner's money, but supported themselves from the money they earned. Yet for every member who made it into the biographical research guides such as the *Women's Who's Who of America* or *Notable American Women*, there is at least one member who has become nearly impossible to find. Furthermore, while it has not been too difficult to discover how members stood on political issues such as suffrage, it has been much harder to uncover how they earned their rent money.

In the first few years of Heterodoxy, several of the members who later achieved a measure of fame were still too young to have done anything to put them into the record books. Helen Hull was still an English instructor at Wellesley, before gaining a position on the Columbia University faculty. Her early short stories revealed little promise of the twenty-five books and numerous short stories she would eventually write. As a local San Francisco reporter, Bessie Beatty did not become well-known until publication of *The Red Heart of Russia*, an account of her experiences in the thick of the 1917 Russian Revolution. Agnes de

In a Russian Trench

Bessie Beatty

Mille was still a schoolgirl, not a famous choreographer, and the novelist Ida Wylie was still enjoying what she later described as her "soulful Teutonic period" in Germany.

Still, most of the other members had enjoyed a good education, which helped prepare them for their later careers. The one great exception was Rose Pastor Stokes, who had only two years of elementary school before going to work in a cigar factory. Nevertheless, her limited formal education was strongly supplemented by both her reading and the Jewish cigarmakers' tradition of paying someone to read aloud to them as they worked.[3] Before she was fifteen, she was writing poems and working as a journalist for the Yiddish-language *Jewish Daily News*. Other women from poor and working class families valued an education enough to work their way through college if they couldn't get enough scholarship money to cover their expenses. Both of Katharine Anthony's parents were teachers. As a child growing up in the little town of Roseville, Arkansas she was an avid reader. After attending Peabody Normal College on a two-year scholarship, she taught school until she had saved enough for a year's advance study in Germany. Later still as a scholarship student at the University of Chicago, Katharine earned her doctorate.

Crystal Eastman's mother was a minister and a feminist. When she was just fifteen, Crystal was sure that she would work for a living rather than be supported financially by another human being. While studying

Crystal Eastman

for her law degree at New York University, she ran the recreation center in Greenwich Village five nights a week, eating her meals in a local settlement house. Katharine Anthony and Crystal Eastman worked together for several years writing reports on women's issues at the social-minded Russell Sage Foundation, long before they both joined Heterodoxy. Their bureaucratic jobs paid the rent while they worked on their own writing and political interests in their spare time.

At a time when a college education was still considered unusual for women, most of the members had at least some college. Doctorates were earned by Helen Hull, Elsie Clews Parsons, Leta Hollingworth, Grace Potter and Katharine Anthony. Crystal Eastman, Inez Milholland, Ida Rauh and Helen Arthur were all lawyers, although only Milholland and Arthur practised for any length of time. Marion B. Cothren passed the New York state bar in 1908, and used her legal background as a stepping-stone to a public service career. Crystal Eastman's roommate, Ida Rauh, seemed to have the most casual approach to her legal qualifications. Like Helen Arthur (who left the law for the more exotic delights of managing beautiful actresses and the Neighborhood Playhouse), Ida found the attractions of the stage and her work as an actress with the Provincetown Players far outweighed the more mundane daily tasks of the law.

Inez Haynes Irwin

For all their intelligence and ability, these women were expected to forget their ambitions and years of schooling as they reached their twenties. Society's dictates on what was a "normal" and acceptable life for American women narrowed to marrying a man, raising a family, and settling down to an existence lived mainly as an adjunct to other's lives once they left college. There were few places open for the career-minded woman in male-dominated America before World War I. Yet most of Heterodoxy's members refused to allow themselves to become only a male appendage with little opportunity for a life of their own. The difficulties encountered by women who persisted in trying to establish a profession were movingly described by Inez Haynes Gillmore [Irwin] in several 1912 articles published in *Harper's Bazaar*. The articles were titled "Confessions of an Alien" because:

> For several years now I have felt myself alien to this world, and alien not because of race and color, but alien because of changing economic conditions. It seems to me that . . . I hang in a void midway between two spheres—the man's sphere and the woman's sphere. A professional career . . .puts me beyond the reach of the average woman's duties and pleasures. The conventional limitations of the female lot put me beyond the reach of the average men's duties and pleasures. . . . The duties and pleasures of the average woman bore and irritate. The duties and pleasures of the average man interest and allure. . . . I soon found that it was a feeling which I shared with the majority of my kind. I have never met a man who at any time wanted to be a woman. I have met few women who have not at some time or other wanted to be men.[4]

As Christopher Lasch has stated, this "cry of despair" was the "common complaint of a certain kind of American woman" from the turn of the century to the First World War—"the middle-class woman of intellectual ambitions."[5] Women increasingly felt the need for an independent life outside of the typical American home and family. The opportunties for them to fulfill that need were limited, however. It took a great deal of fancy economic footwork for a woman to stay financially independent before World War I.

Heterodoxy members' careers covered a large spectrum of professions and fields, but the three largest groups center around writing and journalism, and the theater. There was also a small minority of professional women who pursued careers in the medical, psychological, legal and educational fields.

One of the most popular early jobs of Heterodoxy members was as teachers, though most went on to later careers in other endeavors. Many Heterodoxy women taught at various times in their lives, in environments ranging from the New York public school system (Henrietta Rodman and Sarah Splint) to Arkansas high schools (Katharine Anthony); from Briarfield Junior College in New York (Florence Woolston Seabury) to Wellesley College (Helen Hull and Katharine Anthony) and Columbia University (Elsie Clews Parsons, Helen Hull, and Leta Hollingworth).

Teaching had, of course, long been considered a "natural" career for women's "maternal instincts." By 1900, the majority of elementary and high school teachers were poorly paid women, more often than not unmarried. On the college and university level, the percentage of women teachers decreased dramatically as the prestige and pay rose. Not that teachers on any level were wealthy: Leta Hollingworth's husband earned $1,000 a year as a full-time Columbia University professor during his early years there, and colleges were notorious for consistently paying women instructors and professors lower wages than men earned. Granted, $1,000 was worth a lot more in 1910, but even then, it was a fairly low wage for an educated or business person.

A few members devoted their working lives to education, though none matched the dramatic role Henrietta Rodman played as devil's advocate in the New York schools. She formed the Feminist Alliance in the Village to fight the New York City Board of Education for the right of married teachers to retain their jobs, as well as the right of teachers to return to work after bearing children. The policy of the Board of Education in 1914 was "not to hire married women unless they had been separated from their husbands for at least three years" or their husbands had died.[6] The Feminist Alliance fought the rules in court and through picketing until they won. She was fired as a high school vocational counselor but was eventually reinstated and went to work for a teacher's union. Beyond that, Henrietta Rodman was an original with many followers, and a beloved member of the Village community. Long after her untimely death in 1923 at age forty-five of a cerebral tumor, Henrietta was remembered as a woman who

> explained sex to her high-school girls; she agitated for simpler and saner dress. She wore a loose-flowing gown that looked like a meal sack, and yet did not conceal the trim lines of her body. She wore sandals . . . making the queer, brown socks visible. Her hair was cropped years before the other Village girls dared bob theirs. She did not wear her hat but carried it, dangling it in her nervous, beautiful hands. Once, she decided that she must be a nudist. She practised it at her home, and received vistors in her birth costume. But she was not comfortable and soon gave it up.[7]

Heterodoxy job-holders often felt enormous pride at the sight of their paycheck. Zona Gale wrote:

> When I received my first weekly pay envelope, containing fifteen dollars, I drew pictures on it showing me in the act of getting it at the cashier's window, and mailed it, contents and all, to my parents. It wasn't that they needed the money,. But I was like a dog that wants to bring every treasure, every "find" to show to the person he loves best.[8]

The delightful feeling of not having to depend on father, husband, or other kinfolk for their own spending money was invariably intoxicating. Once a Heterodite had enjoyed the sensation of her own paycheck, she was seldom content to return to receiving an allowance from a related male. Nevertheless, jobs open to women without prejudice were difficult to find. For immigrant, Catholic, Jewish and Black women, the blatantly racist job discrimination that predominated New York's employment practises made it nearly impossible to find decent work paying a living wage. Heterodoxy's single Black member, Grace Nail Johnson, came from a well-to-do Harlem family. Her unusual financial security, as well as her marriage to the poet James Weldon Johnson allowed her to work without pay for the National Association for the Advancement of Colored People and the American Women's Voluntary Service (which she left in protest during World War II over their racial segregation of bandage-rolling volunteers in Harlem).[9] She became well-known as a Harlem hostess and for organizing many literary social events during the Harlem Renaissance. Grace Johnson was fortunate that she did not to have to look for work to put food on her family's table, as countless other Black women were forced to do. She would have been hard put finding intellectual or organizational work befitting her talents.

Earning money through the use of their pens and rickety Remington typewriters was the most profitable occupation for most Heterodoxy women. Over half the members worked as press agents, editors, public relations agents for theaters and actors, playwrights, and radio or movie script writers. They wrote fiction and non-fiction on a variety of subjects for newspapers, magazines, and book publishers. Heterodites wrote not simply as a means of communication and expression, but because they needed the money, no matter what their regular professions might be. Writing markets were plentiful and hungry for talented writers who could be relied on to fill the empty pages between covers, especially in New York where America's major magazines and book publishers were located. The pay was comparatively generous too, particularly after a writer's reputation was established and her faithful readers began eagerly awaiting her next article, short story, or novel.

Name identification was particularly tricky for women writers. A woman writer might find it more profitable to hide her sex behind a male pen name, or use her academic title and first inital to become a sexually anonymous and seemingly more authoritive Dr. F. Maule, instead of Dr. Frances Maule. Another problem was society's traditional practice of erasing a woman's maiden name in favor of her husband's upon marriage. Ruth Hale organized the Lucy Stone League, named after the nineteenth-century feminist leader who refused to give up her "maiden" name simply because tradition said she must take her husband's name. Many women agreed with Ruth Hale and Fannie Hurst, who found it repugnant to be asked to lose their names upon marrying. For women writers and actors, name recognition was money in the bank. A name change like Inez Haynes Gillmore's after her marriage to Will Irwin (making her overnight into Inez Haynes Irwin, an unknown writer) confused her readers and editors, and may have resulted in a loss of income before her public rediscovered her new persona. Think of the identification problem faced by Florence Guy Woolston Seabury or Mabel Dodge Luhan, who kept adding new husbands' names to the discarded husband's. A marital-minded woman like Mabel, with four husbands, could soon end up with little room left on her stationary for much more than her own extended name.[10]

But they didn't just write for the money. Many felt the urgent need to speak from their own experience, and no longer be quiet, inarticulte women in life's background. The feeling of being on the front lines, experiencing life at its fullest, as men always seemed to be able to do, was certainly why journalism held such a strong appeal. Heterodite journalists included Bessie Beatty, Anne O'Hagen Shinn, and Katherine Leckie. Rose Pastor Stokes wrote for the *Jewish Daily News*, *Pravda* and the *Daily Worker*, Rheta Childe Dorr and Rose Young for the *New York Evening Post*, and Mary Heaton Vorse for the Hearst syndicated newspapers. Vorse's books and articles on working class people and the effects of strikes on their families and relationships were well-known for accurate first-hand details. "Any labor trouble found Mary immediately on the spot, and between strikes, she was always speeding on an important assignment to Europe," wrote Inez Haynes Irwin. Heterodoxy knew that she "was one of our members who was always somewhere else."[11]

The other writers in Heterodoxy were equally fluent in writing magazine articles one month and a full-length novel or non-fiction book the next. Their work ranged from purely popular romantic love novels like those of Alice Duer Miller to the elegantly written sociological textbooks of Elsie Clews Parsons; from the love and sin "women's novels" of Fannie Hurst to the monumental four-volume autobiography of Mabel Dodge Luhan and the women's history biographies of Katharine Anthony. Doris Stevens and Inez Haynes Irwin wrote impassioned histories of the women's suffrage movement, while Florence Woolston Seabury and Rose Young were editors of the *Women Voter*, official publication of the Woman Suffrage Party. As noted earlier, Helen Hull wrote an early short story and two novels with strong lesbian overtones and content before switching in the 1920s to novels about more conventional heterosexual family life and marriage. Eventually, she even wrote two mystery novels, winning the Dodd/Mead award for best mystery written by a college professor for *A Tapping in the Wall* in 1960. Some of her best-read articles were on the subject of writing itself, published for those wishing to learn the nuts and bolts of the craft. This grew out of her work as an English instructor at Columbia as well as her leadership role in the Author's Guild. Zona Gale was labeled a "regional" writer, a misnomer most often placed by New York-based critics on novelists who identify their plots and characters in a geographical locality other than New York City. She began her writing career with romantic poetry and fiction, but gained a vast public through her "Friendship" novels based in a small Wisconsin town. She moved on eventually to realistic novels about the underside of small-town life. Her later work took on an almost mystical tone before her death in 1938.

Paula Jakobi's album inscription that began this chapter continued on to say:

> Where was I? O yes. Marie.
> How we have nagged her because she doesn't sign her name
> To a book, or a poem or a play or something.

What does she do anyway?
She has only a genius for friendship.
She only throws her great motherheart open
To us all.[12]

In 1926, Marie Jenney Howe surprised everyone (not the least, herself) by leaving husband Fred behind to manage the homefront without her, and took up residence at 20 Rue Jacob, Paris. She may have been recuperating from an illness. Fola La Follette and her husband, playwright George Middleton, had stayed at 20 Rue Jacob through most of 1920 to 1922, with the famous "Amazon of Letters" lesbian resident, Natalie Barney. They may have arranged it so that Marie Howe could enjoy the sumptous meals provided by Natalie's cook, Marie, while doing the basic research that resulted in her 1927 biography, *George Sand: The Search for Love.* Perhaps the lesbian environment of Natalie Barney's home and her research on a woman who knew the pleasure of loving a woman gave Marie Howe the courage to dedicate her first book not to her husband, but to her close friend and probable lover, Rose Young. All of Marie's self-doubts came out during her solitary research. In a condolence letter to Fola upon the death of Senator La Follette, Fola's father, Marie wrote:

> I am feeling homesick today—Perhaps it is because my thoughts have dwelt on you so much. Do you remember when you came back from France I had just lost my mother, and the house at Easthampton was so full of her that I couldn't stand it and rushed back to Harmon. I still feel that I can never bear to . . . see that house where she died.
>
> If I continue to feel homesick I shall go back. . . . I have no one to talk to. Marie gets my dinner and I do the rest. Marie is an old dear but we don't talk much. She gets Miss Barney's dinner at 8 and rushes mine in ahead. I find it so depressing to be alone so much, as all my friends have gone.
>
> I have profited by my solitude by writing an article on George Sand. But now that it is typed I see how dreadfully poor it is, so I think I shall have to do it all over. . . . I guess I'd better make up my mind that I can't do something I've never learned to do. I've read such a lot on George Sand. But I don't know how to write it. Poor domestic Marie, trying to write, it's impossible.[13]

Much as she doubted her ability to write, Marie continued to work on the biography of Sand, "an Old Girl who got up against the New Girl's problem." (as Lincoln Steffens put it). "It was more impossible in her day than in ours and yet she solved it."[14] Dissatisfied with biographies on Sand written by men, Marie seems to have decided that if she wanted a good feminist biography, she would have to write it herself. Yet the entire writing process terrified her.

Her close friend, Lincoln Steffens, tried to reassure Marie Howe as the book was close to completion.

> . . . I must explicitly write what I so often say of your book: that it is so well written, that it is fresh prose, that it is something r•w in literature.
>
> Another thing: you seem to dread the proofreading for little

things. If you wish me to, I will read your galleys, willingly; and you should ask other friends to read them, too. You can call upon your friends as well as let them forever call upon you. Never thought of that, did you![15]

When *George Sand: The Search for Love* was finally published in 1927, Marie Howe was surprised that it was so well-received by critics and the reading public. She wrote to Fola La Follette:

Today I received my first letter from a stranger in response to my book. She found her own self in George. Somehow when I was sitting here alone working, always tired, always depressed and full of doubts, I never realized that I was writing a sort of letter to a woman living in a hotel in Scranton, Pa. These letters should come to us while we are working and need confidence. It is the wrong way around. But you gave me your encouragement at the right time, bless you, and you will never know how it helped. I will try to tell you sometime. I was ashamed really to admit how low I was in my mind.[16]

Yet Marie Howe earlier had written a satire on the anti-suffrage arguments, and knew that it had sold very well and been well used in political debates around the country.[17] Still, her inner doubts ran deep, and only her knowledge of its importance drew her to complete a second and final book: a translation of *George Sand's Journal* in 1929.[18] In the few letters of hers that have surfaced, it is easy to see that Marie Howe was a natural writer, insightful, with a warm, easy style. It is our loss that she never believed in herself. As Tillie Olson notes in *Silences*, lack of confidence is one of the largest stumbling blocks for women writers.[19]

Other Heterodoxy writers sometimes found themselves silenced not because they felt they couldn't write, but because no one would publish their work. Charlotte Perkins Gilman's ideas were so advanced for her time that few of her articles on socialism and feminism were accepted for publication. So she decided to publish her own magazine, *The Forerunner*, which lasted for seven years. It appeared

each month from November 1906 through December 1916, beginning with 'no capital except a mental one,' and ending when Gilman decided that she had said what had wanted to. She wrote every line of the thirty-two page magazine, including the few advertisements she tolerated for a short while. . . . Each year two books were serialized; the full seven-year run of *The Forerunner* equaled in pages twenty-eight full-length books.[20]

Gilman's *Herland*, a feminist utopian fantasy novel which first appeared in *The Forerunner* in 1915, was one of two feminist novels of an all-woman society invaded ("discovered") by white males written by a Heterodite. The earlier novel was Inez Haynes Irwin's *Angel Island*, which created quite a stir in 1914.[21] Both novels are concerned with the clash of white males misconceptions of how "women really are" against the authors's feminist vision of what women freed from male constraints could become.

Several Heterodoxy women made their livings at least partly as editors. They plied their trade at a great variety of publications in the large

New York periodical market. While Crystal Eastman helped edit *The Masses* and *The Liberator*, Mabel Potter Daggett was editing women's magazines such as *The Delineator*. Rose Young was an editor of *The Woman Citizen* and literary adviser for several New York publishers, while Sarah Splint worked as juvenile editor for several publications.

Inez Haynes Irwin named one of the reasons why writing attracted so many women:

> To me . . . it was highly important. It helped me live in a world in which I found so many problems agonizing to ponder and impossible to solve. Moreover it made life, itself, as spectacular and colorful as though I lived inside a bubble. . . . The writing of those words made all other occupations seem worthless. . . . For there is something incalculably precious about one's own experience.[22]

Radio broadcasting offered Heterodites a new communications outlet, one which gained importance as the years wore on. Bessie Beatty and Mary Margaret McBride began as newspaper journalists. In 1934, during a particularly down-and-out time of her time, McBride was offered the opportunity to host a fifteen minute "women's program" called *Martha Deane* on WOR, New York. After three weeks of making up complicated stories about her large fictional radio family, Mary Margaret McBride stopped in the middle of a broadcast and announced:

> Oh, what's the use? I can't do it! I'm mixed up again with all those grandchildren I've invented. I'm not a grandmother! I'm not a mother. I'm not even married. I made that up and it doesn't sound real because it isn't. The truth is I'm a reporter who would like to come here every day and tell you about places I go, people I meet. Write me if you'd like that. But I can't be a grandmother any more![23]

From then on, her daytime radio show directed to women's domestic interests and human interest stories became so popular that 30,000 fans (including Eleanor Roosevelt) attended the Madison Square Garden party which celebrated her tenth anniversary on radio. When her show was expanded to forty-minutes a day, her mail reached 5,000 letters a day during World War II. McBride's business manager was her longtime lover and friend, Stella Karn. Stella made sure that every *Mary Margaret McBride* show was recorded for history, and arranged for the show to be broadcast from McBride's apartment.[24] Later, Mary Margaret McBride helped Bessie Beatty break into the radio medium by having her as guest hostess on her show. Other Heterodites such as Fannie Hurst, Helen Westley and Alice Duer Miller often appeared as guests discussing their new books or plays on both women's programs.

Lou Rogers began her working career as a physical education teacher, then switched to illustrating children's books and drawing scathing political cartoons such as the examples reprinted in this book from *The Birth Control Review*. By the 1920s, she was also a radio personality on an animal care program directed at the Saturday morning children's audience. She illustrated a sort of newsletter sent to listeners, and drew cartoon verses called "Gimmicks" for *The Ladies Home Journal*.

Heterodites found the theater a wonderful outlet for their talents and

LAWS CONTROLLING
WOMENS' BODIES

THE
STATE

LOU ROGERS

HER LEGAL STATUS

views. Vida Sutton wrote women's suffrage plays. Paula Jakobi wrote at least one play, entitled *Chinese Lily*, while Rose Pastor Stokes' plays were produced by the Washington Square Players. The most famous Heterodoxy playwright, Susan Glaspell, wrote avant-garde plays for the Provincetown Playhouse. She and her husband George Cram Cook helped to start the summer theater group in Provincetown, Massachusetts. Since many of the Greenwich Villagers spent their summer vacations in Provincetown, the new theater group began to put on their plays during the winter in a Village theater. One of her most-produced plays was *Suppressed Desires*, a satire about the new trend for psychoanalysis that had taken over the Village. The theater group did not become known outside of the Village and Provincetown until they began to produce the plays of a little-known playwright named Eugene O'Neill. Soon, they had gained a faithful and growing audience of New Yorkers, who attended, reviewed, and talked as much about Susan Glaspell's plays as Eugene O'Neill's.

The other two theater groups in Greenwich Village which eventually became famous for their lively brand of theater were the Washington Square Players and the Neighborhood Playhouse. Both were more avant-garde, adventurous and a bit amateurist compared to Broadway productions. Their plays tended to be satires on politics, feminism, and sexual freedom. Though the acting was often poor in the early days, reflecting the varied skills of untrained Villagers, the plays were realistic, and soon began drawing New York's theater-going social set down to the Village.

Helen Westley joined Lawrence Langner and other Liberal Club members in organizing the Washington Square Players. Acting mostly character roles, Westley became one of the talented and professional Players, appearing in almost every play they produced. Her dramatic appearance, "dressed rather like a femme fatale—coal-black hair and black, slinky dresses," helped her look "a little like [the cartoonist] Charles Addams' young witch."[25] Westley also helped form the Theater Guild in 1918, and was on the board of directors for fifteen years. She was an excellent example of not only the vitality of so many early Heterodoxy members, but of the changes created by the advancing decades. In 1934, at the age of 59, Helen Westley left for Hollywood to become a movie actress, completing over thirty films before her death eight years later. Her films included *Showboat, Heidi,* and *Rebecca of Sunnybrook Farm.* Margaret Wycherly, another theatrical Heterodite, also left the Broadway stage for a better-paying Hollywood career. Her best-known roles were as Gary Cooper's mother in the 1941 *Sergeant York,* as well as with Spencer Tracy and Katherine Hepburn in *Keeper of the Flame* (based on Heterodite I.A.R. Wylie's novel of the same name), along with sixteen other films.

Margaret Wycherly

A great love for all involved with the theater convinced Helen Arthur to abandon her active law practice and change her career in mid-stream. She volunteered as a drama critic for a small magazine in order to get free theater tickets. Helen Arthur became a press agent, then a theaterical manager for many actresses, including the reknowned Mrs. Patrick Campbell. Helen established her own firm called Actors-Managers, Inc. with her partner and probable lover, Agnes Morgan. Among other plays, in 1928 they produced *Maya,* a play about prostitution that was closed after two weeks by the District Attorney's office on grounds of immorality. Helen Arthur and Agnes Morgan met through their mutual work with Greenwich Village's Neighborhood Playhouse from 1915 through the mid-1920s. From then on, they were inseparable, providing Helen Arthur with a more satisfactory relationship than she had enjoyed briefly in 1906-1907 with social settlement founder Lillian Wald.[26]

(from New York Public Library)

Helen Arthur and friends backstage at the Grand Street Follies (1927)

While Heterodoxy members frequented the theatrical performances of all three Village groups, and faithfully read each other's articles and books, the members who most benefited financially from their club membership were the business and and professional women. Heterodoxy members consulted Dr. Beatrice Hinkle for Jungian psychoanalysis or Grace Potter for a more Freudian viewpoint. Many bought their stocks and bonds from Kathleen de Vere Taylor or Elizabeth Cook in the great Wall Street investment craze of the 1920s. At the time of the stock-market crash in October 1929, Taylor was manager of an all-women employees brokerage firm which dealt only with women customers. "Not one tear did I see during all the time the market was at its worst," she later said. "No crowd of men under pressure ever could show up as better sports."[27] Good sports they may have been, but I've often wondered how many Heterodites lost their hard-earned savings in the crash. The all-woman brokerage suffered such heavy losses that it was forced to close in 1931. Although Kathleen Taylor soon found work in other firms, she could not afford to retire until 1947, when she was seventy-four years old. In an era before pension plans and Social Security became the norm, many women had only their savings to rely on for

Kathleen deVere Taylor

their elderly years. Being an old woman has never been easy, yet it was far more difficult then than now. Even for professional or other self-supporting women who could earn enough to live on in their youth and middle-age, a lifetime of free-lance writing or working in a profession or business still often left women without adequate financial means on which they could retire. Poverty and dependence upon relatives for handouts was (and sadly, still is) a common end for many women, whether they had worked throughout their lives or not. Few managed to save much of their earnings. Actress Helen Westley, one of the more financially fortunate Heterodites, thought of a unique way to insure her savings.

> Helen placed all her earnings, which were considerable in her later years, in the savings banks, and carried her bankbooks at all times on her person. "Good Heavens, Helen!" said Edna Ferber one evening . . . "What are those large lumps on your legs?" "My savings bankbooks," said Helen, "I keep them in my stockings." "But why? asked Edna. "They're worth about seventy thousand dollars," replied Helen. "I couldn't possibly leave them anywhere else."[28]

Heterodoxy followed the professional careers of its better-known members with avid interest and pride. Though few recall their accomplishments today, Leta Hollingworth, Elisabeth Irwin, Elsie Clews Parsons and Dr. Sara Josephine Baker were pioneers in their fields. Leta Hollingworth was an educational psychologist, whose professional career was made more difficult by her marriage in 1908 to a low-income college professor. Her

> time and energy were chiefly consumed by housework, cooking,

dressmaking, mending, washing, ironing, making her own hats and suits and endless other domestic duties in the frugal apartment home. Almost always she effectually stifled her own eager longing for intellectual activity like that of her husband. . . . She led her solitary life in the meagerly furnished quarters. . . . once in a while she would unexpectedly and for no apparent cause burst into tears.[29]

Already a college graduate, she returned to college when the family finances permitted and earned her doctorate from Columbia University. She specialized in "exceptional children," both mentally retarded and gifted intellectually. Inez Irwin recalled that, "One of the most interesting talks she ever gave to Heterodoxy was an account of a class of high I.Q. children whose careers she managed to follow for twenty years."[30]

Hollingworth often discussed educational theories with progressive educator Elisabeth Irwin, founder of the experimental Greenwich Village "Little Red Schoolhouse" in 1921. Both women were interested in helping children learn as easily as possible and to the best of their abilities. Irwin's school was so successful that when the Board of Education decided to close her school during the depression, Village parents paid for it to remain open as a private school under community control. "The Little Red Schoolhouse" was nationally recognized for its program of "intellectual development based directly upon realistic concrete experience."[31] The school, which still flourishes alongside the newer Elisabeth Irwin High School, was one of the first schools in the country to extend the traditional classroom beyond the four walls to the entire city, through field vists and other innovative programs.

Elsie Clews Parsons became famous for her feminist based textbook on *The Family* (1906), which took an anthropological and sociological view of that familiar institution. Her own family experience as the mother of four children and partner in a fairly satisfactory companionate marriage served as background for her academic observations. Nevertheless, her book became highly controversial for its advocacy of trial marriage and other feminist beliefs. As a professor at the New School for Social Research, she taught young Ruth Benedict, who later gained fame for her own work in anthropology. Parson's meticulous and often brilliant work in Southwestern Native American cultures in her later life added to her reputation as one of America's most observant anthropologists.

In the early years of Heterodoxy, possibly its most publicly known New York City member was Dr. Sara Josephine Baker. "Jo," as she much preferred to be called, left us one of the best, most insightful and entertaining autobiographies of the many written by Heterodites. Her book, *Fighting for Life* (1939), brims with passages about the difficulties she overcame to become a physician at the turn of the century. A tomboy who was an "enthusiastic baseball player and trout-fisher," Jo spent much of her childhood trying to "make it up to Father for being a girl." Born into a wealthy family in Poughkeepsie, New York, she was "thoroughly trained in the business of being a woman." Her family assumed she would attend her mother's college, Vassar, after which she was expected to "get married and raise a family and that would be that."[32] However, when she was sixteen, her father and only brother died within three months of each other. Her father's savings turned out to be poorly invested, leaving very little money to support his widow and two daughters.

> It was immediately evident that somebody would have to get ready to earn a living for all three of us—my mother, my sister, who had always been delicate and a semi-invalid, and myself. I considered myself elected. It was a hard struggle to give up Vassar but there was not enough money left to pay for that and for any additional preparation for a professional life![33]

The single-minded and determined young woman was permitted to withdraw five thousand dollars from the family's meager remaining savings. She enrolled in Elizabeth and Emily Blackwell's Women's Medical College in New York City, graduating in 1898. After her internship at the New England Hospital for Women and Children, she returned to New York and set up private practice, earning only $185 the first year. In order to supplement her income, she passed a Civil Service examination for the Department of Health, becoming a medical inspector for thirty dollars a month. She was assigned to an area known as "Hell's Kitchen," the worse slum in the city at that time, and proceeded to do the unthinkable. Unlike the majority of male medical inspectors, she actually did the tasks she was assigned, instead of following the usual practice of working as little as possible and faking records of false home visits. Dr. Baker acquired many enemies in the New York City Health Department by diligently putting in six hours a day after seeing her own patients. Her reports on the appalling conditions she found and the desperate needs of the immigrant families, particularly the mothers and children, helped push through the creation of the Child Hygiene Bureau. Jo Baker became its first director in 1908.

> . . . New York's infant mortality rate . . . soared as high as 1,500 weekly during the summer months. In 1908 she designed an experiment aimed at reducing this shocking toll. With a team of thirty trained nurses, she combed a preselected East Side district, populated primarily by Italian immigrants, where she taught such simple principles of child care as breast feeding (to avoid the hazards of the then unpasteurized bottled milk), ventilation, bathing, and proper clothing. By the end of the hot summer, infant deaths in the district had dropped 1,200 from the previous year, while the mortality rate in other areas showed no significant change . . . .
> Lacking precedents, at a time when preventive medicine was still little known, she established her own.[34]

Dr. Baker became justifibly famous for her efforts on behalf of children's health. Many thousands of babies had a fighting chance at survival, and the possibility of growing up with better health, teeth and eyesight. Retiring in 1923, she continued to work as a consultant to the United States Department of Labor Children's Bureau as well as other state and local agencies, until her death in 1945.

Compared to women in other countries, the business and professional women in America after the First World War were living the good life. Australian-English novelist Ida A.R. Wylie wrote that she left England in the 1920s to work in America for very good reasons.

> Looking wistfully across the Atlantic, I saw that there were professional women who made a good thing out of life, mainly because they made a good living. They could afford to dress well, eat well, and feel well. . . . Even though there are relatively few high-salaried women, there are enough of them to set a high standard of living for "women on their own." The drooping English spinster, stuck fast in the lower-salary brackets, has for an American equivalent a well-dressed upstanding woman of the world who knows her vintages. It's not all a matter of money. The spirit counts even more.[35]

Nevertheless, even though the opportunities for working women to support themselves were enhanced during the 1910s and 1920s, most of the improvements were only on the surface level. "Women were paid less, had fewer important jobs, and faced discrimination in appointments and promotions. They had to be better prepared and have more unusual qualifications than men to secure the same opportunities."[36] Furthermore, little or nothing had changed for women who were not White-Anglo-Saxon-Protestant (WASP), highly educated and/or extremely talented. Although there were many Jewish women in Heterodoxy, only popular novelist Fannie Hurst attained the widespread fame and financial wealth that several of the WASP members enjoyed. As for Grace Nail Johnson, the only Black Heterodite, she saw clearly that the more life seemed to improve for the majority of whites, the more it stayed the same for most Black Americans, especially when it came to economic rewards and employment hiring practices. Her active involvement in the National Association for the Advancement of Colored People (NAACP) was an attempt to change the old racist ways of America's standard "last hired, first fired" attitudes towards Black and other minority workers.

Other Heterodites continued to try to improve working women's conditions and salaries through their articles in leading periodicals and newspapers, while still working for the political organization of women into labor unions. It was an uphill battle against huge odds. This was especially dispiriting to many of the oldest members who had worked so diligently for suffrage, with at least a partial hope that the vote would be a key to a better world for women. Sara Josephine Baker's keen disappointment was clear in her autobiography.

> . . . I do not think that many women have been the success they might well be. It is still a man's world. The vote did not bring us either full emancipation or full opportunity. We still have plenty of indirect influence but little that is direct. We have made some gains but we have also suffered many losses.[37]

Politically as well as economically, Dr. Baker was right. Women *had* "suffered many losses." As J. Stanley Lemons documents so well in *The*

Woman Citizen, from about 1925 until 1933 when the New Deal and Franklin D. Roosevelt came into power, women in America saw "the end of the flush times of social feminism and the beginning of the famine years."[38] Heterodoxy members as well as other feminists "entered a defensive stage. Instead of being able to count the number of reforms won, they often had to be satisfied with preventing mischief." Rightwing, red-baiting conservatives who saw a Communist behind every labor and social reform ruled the day. Feminists found themselves faced with "discouraging judicial decisions, legislative conservatism, and continued attacks from the right."[39]

Still, many women in the twenties and thirties, individually and collectively, continued "to work for political, social, economic, and industrial reform. They helped develop the issues and proposals from which the New Deal would grow."[40] While some Heterodites gave up the political arena for more concentrated personal battles to survive economically, others faced the 1930s with undimmed vigor despite their increasing age. Myran Louise Grant was one of those. In the 1920 club album, she toasted Marie Jenney Howe with a wish that was fulfilled by many Heterodites:

> I would drink daily to you, Marie, and to the future of Heterodoxy in spirits of age, labeled "The Older the Bolder," accompanying the draught of rare old vintage with a toast that runs like this: May we prove to be women whose opinions advance a mile with every whitening hair, acquiring them with a certain equanimity, poise, and wide tolerance which are the natural results of an enlightened consciousness. May we discard the caution of youth as year by year we have less and less to lose, therefore less and less that we need fear risking, thus accumulating with time the elderly winters of rashness, recklessness, and a certain splendor of generosity. . . . illustrating by our lives that gray hairs are the banner of adventure. . . .[41]

Footnotes to Chapter 4

1. Paula Jakobi, "Heterodoxy to Marie" club album.
2. Irwin, "Adventures," p. 415.
3. *Notable American Women: 1607-1950*, s.v. "Stokes, Rose Harriet Pastor," by David A. Shannon.
4. Inez Haynes Gillmore, "Confessions of an Alien," *Harper's Bazaar*, April 1912, p. 170.
5. Lasch, p.
6. Sochen, p. 52.
7. Albert Parry, *Garrets and Pretenders* (New York: Dover Pub., 1960, revised edition), p. 270.
8. August Derleth, *Still Small Voice: The Biography of Zona Gale* (New York: D. Appleton Century, 1940), p. 22.
9. *The New York Times*, February 26, 1942.
10. Imagine the trouble and trauma this dilemma has caused women's historians over the years, diligently trying to track down every reference to these women in indexes and biographical sources. Multiply that by 110 Heterodoxy members, and you will understand a bit more of the process that goes into creating a book like this. If you are considering the scholarly life, carefully mull over my heartfelt suggestion to limit your research to never-married women. It leaves a heck of a lot out of women in history, of course, but such a policy will save you countless gray hairs and innumerable headaches.
11. Irwin, "Adventures," p. 416.
12. Paula Jakobi, "Heterodoxy to Marie" club album.
13. Marie Jenney Howe to Fola La Follette, June 20, 1926(?), La Follette Family Papers.
14. Lincoln Steffens to Marie Jenney Howe, December 23, 1925, in Ella Winter and Granville Hicks, eds., *The Letters of Lincoln Steffens*, 2 vols. (New York: Harcourt, Brace & Co., 1938), 2:723.
15. Ibid., 2:796.
16. Marie Jenney Howe to Fola La Follette, October 1927(?), La Follette Family Papers.
17. Marie Jenney Howe, *An Anti-Suffrage Monologue* (New York: National American Women Suffrage Association, 1913).
18. Marie Jenney Howe, *George Sand's Intimate Journal* (New York: John Day, Inc., 1929); Marie Jenney Howe, trans. and ed., with preface by Aurore Sand, *Intimate Journal of George Sand* (New York: Haskell House Pubs., 1975).
19. Tillie Olson, *Silences* (New York: Delta, 1979).
20. Ann J. Lane, "Introduction" to Charlotte Perkins Gilman, *Herland* (New York: Pantheon Books, 1979), pp. v-vi.
21. Inez Haynes Gillmore [Irwin], *Angel Island* (New York: H. Holt & Co., 1914).
22. Irwin, "Adventures," p. 518.
23. Mary Margaret McBride, *Out of the Air: The Most Radio-Active Woman in America* (Garden City, New York: Doubleday, 1960), p. 19.

24. Thus far, these invaluable recordings have not been found. I checked the Museum of Broadcasting for anything related to Heterodoxy members. There was a radio drama about atomic bombs dropped on America, written by Fannie Hurst. An Edward R. Murrow "See It Now" television program has a funny episode with Mary Margaret McBride interviewing an "airliner stewardess" about the freshness of airplane food. But no recordings were found of "The Mary Margaret McBride Show." It grieves me to think that Stella's sense of history which caused her to go to the great trouble of recording her lover's programs was so fruitless. Did they end up in a wastebasket or broken in some rubbish heap? Can you suggest possible places to look?

25. *Notable American Women: 1607-1950*, s.v. "Westley, Helen," by Pat M. Ryan.

26. See Blanche Wiesen Cook, *Women and Support Networks* (New York: Out & Out Books, 1979), pp. 23-27.

27. *New York Times*, November 6, 1949, p. 6.

28. Lawrence Langer, *The Magic Curtain* (New York: E.P. Dutton & Co., 1951), p. 94.

29. Harry L. Hollingworth, *Leta Stetter Hollingworth: A Biography* (Lincoln, Nebraska: University of Nebraska, 1943), p. 98.

30. Irwin, "Adventures," p. 422.

31. *The New York Times*, October 17, 1942, p. 15:1.

32. Baker, pp. 2-12.

33. Ibid., p. 25.

34. *Notable American Women: 1607-1950*, s.v. "Baker, Sara Josephine," by Leona Baumgartner.

35. I.A.R. Wylie, *My Life With George* (New York: Random House, 1940), p. 279. ["George" was Wylie's pet name for her creative muse, a sort of imp that let her know when she was ready to write another novel.]

36. Lemons, *The Woman Citizen*, p. 229.

37. Baker, p. 247.

38. Historical cycles have always fascinated me, but never more so than when I read of those "famine years" just after women got the vote, and compare them to our present civil rights, minority and feminist famine of the Reagan-Falwell years. How hard I yearn to believe that this, too, shall pass, and is nothing more than another painful downward cycle of women's history. Yet, the phrase "history repeats itself" is a fearsome thought—who among us would want much of the twentieth century repeated?

39. Lemons, *The Woman Citizen*, p. 228. [All of this sounds so familiar! Sometimes while researching Heterodoxy, I couldn't tell the difference between reading women's history from the 1920s and reading the daily newspaper, there was such a great similarity between them both.]

40. Ibid.

41. Myran Louise Grant, "Heterodoxy to Marie" club album.

Too Self-Satisfied to Take Notice
Drawn for the Birth Control Review by Lou Rogers

Salutation

Het 'rodiks, yuletide greetings!
At this season of gifts—
Shall I tell you the gifts you bestow on me,
As we sit at the long tables,
And the years slip along?
Gifts intangible and imponderable—,
Yet bright with reality?

For there is no subtler pleasure—
Than to know minds capable——
Of performing the complete act of thought.—
There is no keener joy than to see—
Clear-cut human faces,—
Faces like those men choose—
For coins, and cameos—

Leta S. Hollingworth

Love and Heterodoxy

Dear Marie: I really love you, and I don't know how to make a joke or verse about that. As to Heterodoxy — it is the nicest place I know, and I am proud to be a part of it.[1]

As Elinor Byrns knew when she wrote the above for the 1920 gift album to Marie Jenney Howe, love and affection were serious matters in Heterodoxy. The club was formed in an era of deep changes in the traditional models for human relationships. In Greenwich Village in particular, the options for sexual expression seemed suddenly limitless. Now, a woman could at least consider the choices presented around her before deciding whether or not to obey the old morality she may have grown up hearing. Those choices included whether to enjoy sex with men, women, or both sexes separately or together. A woman could wait until she felt romantic attachment to the other person, or accept the new view that sexual attraction was a perfectly good reason to go to bed with someone, whether you felt you loved them or not. Another decision was whether to wait for the committment of a marriage license before sex, vowing not to sleep with others as long as the maritial ties were in force (or, for gay men and lesbians, living together in a sexually monogamous partnership that carried similiar restrictions, responsibilities, problems and delights as a heterosexual marriage bond); or whether to join in an "open marriage" with the understanding that nobody should feel too out of sorts if either partner slept with others, as long as the primary bond stayed within the marriage. It was really quite confusing. Subtle changes in sexuality and moral attitudes swept in with the new century, gaining strength as new viewpoints were popularized in the magazines and newspapers of the day. These included changes in the role expectations for men and for women, the grip of family ties loosening their hold across America (but especially in metropolitian areas like New York), and the rise in divorce rates. All of these were denounced from the pulpits of America while being discussed favorably in the more liberal periodicals. Urbanization, industralization and the mental and physical upheavals of the First World War accelerated the process of social and sexual upheavals in individual and family relationships. It was a difficult time for most people in their personal lives, no matter whether they feared or welcomed the multitude of choices.

Heterodoxy members' lives were a good reflection of those changes. As Florence Woolston Seabury noted in her playful tabulation of Heterodoxy "Marriage Customs", the members' personal lives divided into "three types of sex relationships" which Seabury labeled "monotonists, varietists, and resistants." The women she called "monotonists" were the members who had "mated young and by pressure of habit and circumstance have remained mated."[2] These were the women who married conventionally just after finishing high school or college, or by their early twenties. They usually had not worked at all outside the home before their marriage, although some may have taught school a couple of years. Raised and socialized in the strongly patriarchal and family-oriented era at the end of the Nineteenth century, these women seldom questioned the basic assumption that they would marry, have several children, and be supported by their husbands. With the morality of their youth denying a woman the right to any sexual relations outside of a ring on her finger and a legal husband in her bed, and with a minimum of economic avenues open to a decent living wage with which to support herself, the late Victorian woman had few reasonable options other than marriage. Moreover, love and marriage were romanticized heavily in the popular magazines and songs of the day. A woman was not considered "fulfilled" until she married and bore children, even though she may have been perfectly content in her own work and pleasures as a single woman. A good example of a highly intelligent woman who accepted society's reasoning was Leta Stetter, who married Harry Hollingworth and left her budding career as a writer and teacher for a life of household drudgery. She acknowledged at the time of her marriage that while "true love is the most uplifting and glorifying of all the passions . . . it is not the only passion."[3] Yet she still accepted her fate of "staying at home eating a lone pork chop" with only occasional periods of depression and discouragement.[4] Even after she finally left the daily household grind to build a strong reputation as an educational psychologist, Leta Stetter Hollingworth was still so socialized that despite her feminist beliefs in the right of the individual to personal freedom and happiness, her husband could state after her death that "subordination of her own aims and needs to the needs of others . . . was steadily characteristic of Leta Stetter, always."[5]

Some Heterodoxy women who married had to go through a period of soul-searching first (as in the case of Marie Jenney Howe), only giving consent after a lengthy period working on their own careers. Crystal Eastman was twenty-nine years old, an independent lawyer living in the anything-goes atmosphere of Greenwich Village for several years when she wrote her brother Max that she was "feeling very scared about getting married." Still, she did it anyway, moving to Milwaukee to live with her new husband, insurance agent Wallace Benedict. Four years later, she divorced him.[6] Her second marriage to English theatrical agent Walter Fuller was apparently mutually satisfying (including the birth of two children). The fact that they shared mutual interests in social causes and radical political beliefs may have strengthened that happiness.[7]

Heterodoxy marital records offer one more example of the club members' uniqueness. Divorce was fairly uncommon in America, although a growing trend after 1920. One study of divorce patterns between 1900-1920 shows that there were four to eight divorces per one thousand marriages. Heterodites, on the other hand, had a 33% divorce rate during those same years.[8] Few members, however, could challenge

Mabel Dodge Luhan's record of three divorces and several love affairs before she settled down in Taos, New Mexico with Antonio Luhan, a Pueblo Indian sculptor.

Florence Seabury stated in her spoof of Heterodite mating practices that "sometimes sheer inertia and the difficulty of unmating keeps the monotonist as such."[9] Arranging a divorce in pre-World War I America was very difficult in most states, even if both parties desired to sever their living arrangement. Usually, adultery had to be proved against one of the partners before the marriage could go to court, much less be dissolved. This was true even if the husband was a wife beater or alcoholic. The economic system supported the traditional marriage, through inequality in wages paid to men and women, as well as the extremely limited and very low-paying occupational choices open to most women. Assuming that a woman had a fairly decent husband, she still often lived vicariously through her husband and family, with their interests and activities becoming more important to her than her own. Divorce (whether or not it was her choice or his) shattered such women, leaving them bewildered and confused about such fundamental questions as what to do with their lives, as well as how much of their personality and daily interests were really their own, and how much acquired by osmosis from their ex-husbands' needs and expectations.

Twenty-four-year-old Charlotte Perkins had a premonition of a "future of failure and suffering" before she married the painter Charles Stetson. After the marriage and birth of a daughter, her premonition seemed to come true.

> Here was a charming home; a loving and devoted husband; an exquisite baby, healthy, intelligent and good; a highly competent mother to run things; a wholly satisfactory servant—and I lay all day on the lounge and cried.[10]

Though the marriage was outwardly a picture of the American dream, Charlotte Perkins Stetson found herself living a nightmare of melancholia and seemingly unreasonable depression. She finally realized that the depression lifted whenever she was able to remove herself from the stifling effects of her enclosed family life. After ten years of marriage, she and Stetson divorced. They remained good friends, since Charlotte felt deeply that neither partner was at fault as much as the institution of marriage as it then existed, and its restraints on women. Six years after her divorce from Stetson, she married her cousin, George Gilman, in 1900, with the understanding that they would not have the traditional type of marriage. Her continuing relationship with her ex-husband and his new wife was as unorthodox for that era as any of her political beliefs. Inez Irwin recalled:

> When she and her first husband parted, she told him that he ought to marry Grace Ellery Channing, a beloved friend to both of them. Ultimately he did marry Grace and that marriage was a perfect one. No more perfect than Charlotte's second marriage, however. . . . Those four remained friends until death parted them. They used to meet weekly. This was the first time that I had ever heard of people who had been married and had become divorced, turning

Elsie Clews Parsons   Grace Nail Johnson

their love and marriage into a great friendship. It seemed to me a
beautiful development.[11]

Some of the Heterodites enjoyed a good marriage the first time
around and never felt the need for a divorce. Elsie Clews Parsons may
have advocated trial marriages in her book *The Family*, but she married
the lawyer Herbert Parsons at age twenty-five, and seemed overall
more satisfied than not. She was not thrilled with his love affairs, and
considered having a few of her own, but doesn't seem to have acted out
the impulse. They differed strongly on pacifist issues, particularly during the First World War, when he served as a United States Army
intelligence officer. Nevertheless, their life together was a good one.

> They shared a love of the outdoors and spent many summers
> hiking, riding, and swimming at a family farm in Lenox, Massa-
> chusetts, where Mrs. Parsons appropriated a small hillside cabin
> for her writing. Since Herbert Parsons was himself a person of
> independent mind he could accept his wife's ways with equan-
> imity.[12]

The Parsons had six children, four of whom survived childhood. This
made them one of the most fertile couples in the Heterodoxy membership. Despite frequent pregnancies and family responsibilities, Parsons
managed to continue her work as an anthropologist, writer, and educator. She was one of the few who were so lucky.

Rose Pastor Stokes was another Heterodoxy member who was unorthodox in both her politics and her marriage. She met her future husband when she went to interview him for her column in the Yiddish
language newspaper, *The Jewish Daily News*. James Phelps Stokes was
a Catholic, a Socialist, and a millionaire working with the University
Settlement in New York City's Lower East Side. The marriage of the ex-

cigar maker Jewish girl reporter and the millionaire Catholic "was hailed by the popular press as a Cinderella match. After a three-month wedding trip abroad, they took an apartment in New York's Russian quarter. . . . They had no children."[13] They had a fairly happy marriage until World War I, when they disagreed over socialism and pacifism. James Phelps Stokes left the Socialist Party never to return, but Rose changed her mind after the Russian Revolution and returned to socialism. The Stokes were divorced in 1925, after years of mutual antagonism. Rose Pastor Stokes remarried in 1927, this time to a language teacher and fellow Communist, Isaac Romaine, but continued to use her first husband's name. She died of cancer six years later.

Grace Nail, the daughter of a prosperous and well-known Black Harlem family, was only in her mid-teens when she first met James Weldon Johnson. He was already in his thirties, assigned to the American charge d'affaires post in Corinto, Nicaragua, as well as a talented published poet. Grace Nail married Johnson when he was home on leave in 1910 and returned with him to Nicaragua. Later, they lived in Johnson's hometown, Jacksonville, Florida, but the blatent racism there was intolerable. ". . .Grace, born and raised in the North, found the adjustment to Southern racial mores difficult and distasteful."[14] They moved to Harlem in New York in 1914, where both became deeply involved in the National Association for the Advancement of Colored People (NAACP) and other progressive causes such as women's suffrage. Their marriage was a blend of mutual interests. Both were friends of Fred and Marie Jenney Howe. Grace Nail Johnson's inscription in the 1920 album speaks of the "great esteem and love that is mine for you."[15] Much later, James Weldon Johnson was asked by Heterodoxy to be one of the few male speakers at the memorial service for Marie Howe in 1934. Apparently, Grace Nail was not one of the women speakers at that service.

On June 26, 1938, the Johnsons were returning from a vacation in Maine, with Grace driving their car in a blinding rainstorm. The car was hit by a train, killing James Weldon Johnson instantly, and injuring Grace severely. "The funeral . . . marked one of the largest in the history of Black Harlem, with over two thousand jammed into Salem Methodist Church."[16]

Grace Nail Johnson recovered but never remarried. Her political activism, racial discrimination protests and Black literary and society parties continued to be reported in the Black press and the *New York Times*, as in the case of her resignation from the American Women's Voluntary Services in 1942 for "unfair racial treatment" in its organizational work in Harlem.[17]

Heterodite novelist Zona Gale seemed to have made the choice to remain single all her life. But at age fifty-three, she unexpectedly married William Breese, a hometown man she had known and admired since childhood. Her extended state of single bliss was influenced by her parent's "intense, indeed possessive, concern for their daughter and her career."[18] Her mother, in particular, attempted to engulf Zona

Zona Gale

Gale's life with a cocoon of care. Both parents were delighted when their only daughter left New York City and returned home to the small town of Portage, Wisconsin, where she had grown up.

After her mother's death, however, Zona Gale began to reach out beyond the tight family circle for warmth and new people to devote herself to—especially young beginning writers. In 1927, before her engagement with Breese, Zona Gale began to support a baby girl named Leslyn. Her father declared he did not want a noisy baby in the family home, so she rented a separate house for her new daughter and the full-time nurse who actually tended the baby. After her marriage, she and her husband legally adopted Leslyn, and "she now found it possible to gratify her frustrated maternal instincts to the full."[19] She became so involved in the baby that she filled notebooks with Leslyn's baby talk and every new sign of growth, giving the task to the nurses when she was away from home. Her marriage and instant motherhood did not curb any of her political or literary interests, however. She continued to speak out on political issues, especially on matters involving Wisconsin state politics, and wrote at a steady pace until her death in 1938 at age sixty-four.

I was surprised that so vital a woman, with many personal interests and avenues of fulfillment, would become such a complusive mother. It seems more understandable if the mother has few activities or interests apart from her family, or a great need to identify with her children's accomplishments. This did not seem to be the case with Zona Gale, but it did seem to be true for Anna George de Mille. After her "terrible" divorce, she "was shattered . . . she was still powerful and active, but her heart, that is, her pride, had been broken. She was a desperate woman."[20] The acute dilemma that Anna George de Mille found herself in was that she had lost her position and identity as a "wife" in a marriage-oriented society, and didn't know what to do with herself for the rest of her life. Although active in her father Henry George's single-tax cause, she never held (nor did she financially need to hold) a paying job. She felt that she had little or no talent on which to build a late-blooming career. Her decision was a sad but understandable one: to live "by proxy" through her daughters, particularly the youngest one, choreographer and dancer Agnes de Mille. As Agnes put it in her autobiography, her mother "married me and as a wedding gift she gave me my career." The daughter felt that a "scapel lay right by her [mother's] caressing hand." Anna George de Mille's interference and constant questions about her daughters' personal lives drove them to evasion and lies in order to preserve any privacy from her "corrosive" intervention. They "endured" their mother "with exhaustion" while at the same time feeling great pity for her situation. Anna George de Mille's daughters were still her most avid interest at her death in 1947.[21]

For all their outspoken belief in new ways of relating to the world and their own position in it, none of these women who practiced "monotony" with men could visualize a future without the traditional framework (sooner or later) of marriage and usually, motherhood. A committment to motherhood was not as common as it had been in an earlier era, however. As Florence Seabury noted, "undoubtedly *Neo-Malthusianism* or *Sangerism* is thoroughly familiar to them." Although Margaret Sanger was angry at Heterodoxy members for not becoming more involved with her birth control, the issue of birth control was certainly very central to most heterosexual members' lives. Sanger spoke at a Heterodoxy meeting in 1914 and reported that she "struck no responsive chord." Sanger found it "unbelievable" that women "could be serious in occupying themselves with what I regarded as trivialities" such as a woman's right to keep her maiden name after marriage and women's "demand for the right to work."[22]

One Heterodoxy member did answer her plea for assistance. Mary Ware Dennett became so identified with the birth control cause that she became almost a rival of Sanger's, after Margaret Sanger was forced to leave the country for several years to avoid arrest under the postal obscenity laws for sending birth control information through the mails. The two women disagreed over the best way to disseminate the information, with Margaret Sanger now advocating that only doctors should handle contraceptive devices and information, while Mary Ware Dennett's Voluntary Parenthood League stood for elimination of all legal restraints so that birth control devices and information would be available to all.[23]

Mary Ware Dennett

Birth control was as much a vital issue to the feminist cause in 1910 as it is today, for the simple reason that it provides the means for women to engage in heterosexual intimacy without fear of unwanted or inconvenient pregnancies. Without such information, Greenwich Village women would not have been able to advocate "free love" beliefs so carefreely, without marriage or a similar economic structure available to provide for all the children that would be produced. For the young Village woman of the 1910s and 1920s, a woman's sexual right to make love with whomever she wished without troubling to get a marriage license beforehand was basic to all her other rights as a human being. Also, without the means to control the consequences of heterosexuality, women could not gain real economic independence, since pregnancy, birth and dependent infants clearly interfered with most jobs and careers. While not directly mentioning birth control, one of Inez Haynes Irwin's recollections of a conversation with another Heterodite reflects the linkage she saw between society's sexual standards for women and a woman's ability to control her own economic destiny.

> A statement of one of our members immediately gave me to think. She was telling simply but frankly the story of her love affair and her marriage. She ended, "But I would not have married him if I had not lived with him for a year to find out whether or not I cared enough for him to marry him." That was the first time I had ever heard any woman make a statement that, in my childhood and girlhood, would have been described as "compromising.". . . in all the plays of the period, some woman was sure to be compromised. But later I reflected with a great surge of feministic triumph that most of the women of Heterodoxy were through their own efforts economically independent. Many of them with established and impregnable reputations. They were as independent of their own "compromising" confessions as any man. That word seems quaint now; it has almost disappeared from common use.[24]

Greenwich Village men enjoyed the emergence of women as free spirited playmates, but found themselves uncomfortable with the complete extent of women's freedom. Hutchins Hapgood saw the Village man as a "victim" whose "property" had been taken away from him, and "no matter what his advanced ideas were, his deeply complex, instinctive, and traditional nature often suffered" from the woman's "full assumption of his old privileges."[25]

Free love in the Village was not "illicit self-indulgence," but instead a "serious ethical undertaking."[26] Living together only so long as they both still cared for each other, the bohemian couples of the Village believed in romantic ideals even more strongly than many conventional small-town Americans. The only sin was living with someone you no longer loved—that was seen as almost a form of prositution. The free love advocates were the "varietists" that Seabury noted in Heterodoxy, "never ceremonially mated but [preferring] a succession of matings."[27] A Villager later recalled:

> In fact, free love soon became so respectable, that no "modern" young man would go out with a girl who was living with another man, with the result that free lovers were usually thrown on each other's company to such an extent that they became bored to distraction with one another and ultimately got married just in order to have a little more freedom.[28]

It was often difficult to know who was married and who was living together in the Village, since so many of the married women were in sympathy with Ruth Hale's Lucy Stone League, and refused to change their "maiden" names after marriage. This led to separate names on the mailbox and confusion (as well as hostility) in hotels while traveling, but not to any loss of respect in their own community, whether they were married or not. Village couples placed a high value on each person's individual freedom, as Fola La Follette's husband George Middleton remembered:

83

When finances permitted, Fola and I had our own secret retreats outside, where neither would intrude on the other. We soon established our own rhythm of life. This left luncheons free for our individual concerns. So we did not have to emulate a friend and her husband, each of whom did what the other wanted on alternate days. On Sundays they did what neither wanted.[29]

The playwright Susan Glaspell's recollections of the Greenwich Village and Provincetown young people of the 1910s and 20s helps to dispute their historical image as "wild Bohemian" types living formless, free spirited lives.

> We were supposed to be a sort of "special" group—radical, wild. Bohemians, we have even been called. But it seems to me we were a particularly simple people, who sought to arrange life for the thing we wanted to do, needing each other as protection against complexities, yet living as we did because of an instinct for the old, old things: to have a garden, and neighbors, to keep up the fire and let the cat in at night. None of us had much money, these were small houses we lived in; [in Provincetown] they had been fishermen's before they were ours. Most of us were from families who had other ideas—who wanted to make money, play bridge, voted the Republican ticket, went to church, thinking one should be like every one else. And so, drawn together by the thing we really were, we were as a new family; we lent each other money, worried through illnesses, ate together . . . talked about our work. Each could be himself, that was perhaps the real thing we did for one another.[30]

Several of the two dozen Heterodites who chose never to marry at all also chose to live the simple life in Greenwich Village and Provincetown. Some of the nearly forty Heterodites for whom I could find no evidence of their marital status also probably lived their lives as single women. These were the women Florence Seabury referred to in the *Marriage Customs* spoof as "resistants," adding that "true resistants are rare." She went on to conclude that many women only pretended to be "resistants" because of repercussions by society against "loose women."[31] Some of the single women undoubtedly experienced heterosexual relations, especially some of the younger generation of Heterodites. A few others were possibly not drawn to intimacy or sexual expression with another human being of either sex, and chose celibacy. They may well have found most of their emotional needs fulfilled through close friendships, while their sexual needs were either self-fulfilled or repressed. Some Heterodite women clearly valued emotional independence from intimate emotional and sexual relationships, for the sake of their individual freedom. Their careers and political activism took a great deal of time and energy, both physical and emotional, leaving little for the satisfaction of other needs.

> When many professional women who had never married reminisced about their lives, they felt little regret. For romantic love and family devotion, they had substituted devotion to a cause and the close friendship of other women. Heterosexuality was not the key to their lives.[32]

It is easy to assume one of two things in writing the history of unmarried women. One is that the woman you are studying was celibate, sexless and unconcerned with that state, living her life in an emotional obilivion with nary a wayward thought. The other assumption is less often made, but becoming more common: if she wore trousers or tailored suits and ties, if she lived even a year or more with another woman, or if she sometimes signed her letters to another woman, "With Love," she must surely have been a lesbian. In the face of so little lesbian history that is easily available, many lesbians ache to believe that most single women (particularly women of accomplishment or politically admirable) of the past were lesbians, or at least, would have been if they *could* have been. And, in truth, those of us who know how many women did indeed live their lives loving other women, often find ourselves wondering who among our cultural heroines *wasn't* a lesbian. While I am one of the first to agree that we should trust our instincts in searching for lesbian history, I also ask for more information (not "proof") of some sort of self-identification as a lesbian or at least as a woman who preferred women friends, if not lovers, before naming a woman to the "possibles" category or adding her to the biographical files in the Lesbian Herstory Archives. She needn't have been proud of it or declared herself publicly (although that would be nice, of course), but it will take more than an affinity for ties or the comfort of trousers to convince me, much as I might feel drawn to her. Certainly we needn't be proud of every lesbian that was ever lived. We may find ourselves repulsed by her racism, her political beliefs, the choices she made in living her life, or any number of other things that went into making her a human being. Nevertheless, I always want to know more, which is why I prefer original letters and documents rather than secondary sources. That is also why I prefer to quote lengthy passages from the women's own words rather than paraphase and sum it up into neat and tidy packages. What I wish always to know is this: did they know?, and did they act on that self-knowledge? And if they didn't, did they still, to all intents and purposes, live their lives as if they had?

Using this sort of definition, Heterodoxy had at least ten lesbian members, three others who knew the powerful pleasures of physical and emotional love between women, and at least eleven members who very probably were lesbians. The lesbians were: Katharine Anthony and her lover, Elisabeth Irwin, Helen Arthur, Dr. Sara Josephine Baker and one of her lovers, Ida Wylie, Myran Louise Grant, Helen Hull, Paula Jakobi, Mary Margaret McBride, and Rose Young. Three other Heterodites had emotional, affectional, and probably sexual relationships with both men and women: Charlotte Perkins Gilman, Marie Jenney Howe and Mabel Dodge Luhan. The "possibles" in need of more research were Edwina Behre, Anne Herendeen, Edna Kenton, Alice Mary Kimball, Virginia Kline, Ellen La Motte, Eleanor Lawson, Frances Maule, Lou Rogers, Kathleen de Vere Taylor, and Gertrude Williams. Twenty-four women-loving-women out of 110 known members: a respectable percentage of Heterodoxy.

While these women indeed enjoyed "close friendships with other women," some of those friendships/relationships included all the traditional male-female marital benefits (such as shared living arrangements; shared expenses and incomes; warm, intimate, often life-long companionship; sexual enjoyment and sometimes raising children) without most of the marital drawbacks (unwanted pregnancies; curtailment of the wive's career and many other freedoms for the sake of the male's ego needs; power abuses by the physically stronger husband who knew he was backed by the law of the land and social custom; etc., etc.). When these women joined their lives together with another woman, they kept honeymoon photograph albums; called each other "sweetheart," "beloved," and "darling;" and generally enjoyed the usual passionate sexual stage that most relationships go through. As the years passed and the physical ardor calmed down, their letters and diaries noted the more mundane events of their active lives—meetings attended, illnesses suffered and (usually) conquered; dinner and weekend guests entertained, disagreements and shared pleasures, as well as the homey coziness and sometimes boredom of everyday life. As these couples matured, most of them earned honors for all their years of dedication to their careers. Occassionally those careers were intertwined, so that both members of the couple shared in the recognition.

When a "devoted companion" sickened and died, leaving her "close friend" behind, many knew well that the newspaper obituaries lied when they proclaimed, "She left no known survivors." The remaining woman grieved openly, while her other old friends attempted to console her. Her life continued on, often alone, going back to the summer place the two of them had once enjoyed so much, caring for the cat and the garden and the daily chores, until one day, she, too, died.

As far as I have been able to tell, none of these women suffered economically in their last years, although most of them who lived past age 65 continued to work. It is possible that they had to work to live; it is also possible that they enjoyed their work so much, it would have seemed like a living death *not* to work. It is also possible that the lesbians planned ahead for retirement a bit more than the heterosexual women, knowing that they could only rely on their own savings during the strong earning years to tide them over old age.

Katharine Anthony and Elisabeth Irwin were one of the two most publicly acknowledged couples. Inez Haynes Irwin described them well:

> They kept house together. Katharine was the author of a generous
> line of brilliant biographies; a wise woman with a philosophic out-
> look and a delicious sense of humor. Elisabeth was a live, warm,
> earthy type with the fine trained mind of the educator. She was an
> iconoclast.[33]

For all the information already mentioned on their political activism and careers, I have only seen a few letters that give glimpses of their personal relationship. They lived together for nearly thirty years in Greenwich Village. In the summers, they enjoyed a summer cottage in

Gaylordsville, Connecticut, where they called themselves "the gay ladies of Gaylordsville."[34] Elisabeth Irwin adopted several children, which the two women jointly raised. She died of cancer in 1942, leaving two young boys in Katharine's care.[35]

Dr. Baker and Ida A. R. Wylie were another Heterodite couple. Both women wrote excellent, entertaining autobiographies in which they described their unconventional tomboyish child hoods, their dislike of the typical male-female relationships they saw around them, and their desires for professional careers and financial independence. They met when Wylie arrived in New York from England after the First World War. Both were members of Heterodoxy in 1920, when the club album was created. Wylie described their first meeting in her autobiography:

> . . . I met Dr. S. Josephine Baker, who it seemed had read Towards
> Morning and yearned to meet the author.
>
> Unfortunately, I had no idea who she was or that she had
> occupied a unique position in the medical world and New York's
> civic life. I had never heard of a baby death rate and certainly did
> not know what she had done with it. So that my opening gambit,
> "Are you still practicing, Dr. Baker?" produced a noticeable chill.
> However, we met again and she forgave me my insular ignorance.
> We drifted into sharing a New York apartment together and years
> later this pleasant house in Princeton where Dr. Louise Pearce of
> the Rockefeller Institute and African sleeping sickness fame
> joined us.[36]

Wylie considered herself "not fitted for matrimony," although she readily admitted that she was "affectionate, a good and faithful friend . . . always generous and sometimes actually unselfish. . . ." With uncommon insight, she acknowledged that her attitude in her personal relationship with Dr. Baker was "faintly masculine . . . I like to be taken care of, to have my clothes mended. . . . My hand held when my head aches . . . in the grand manner I want to be IT." Wylie also admitted that she "disliked children as heartily as I did when I was a child myself."[37] Dr. Baker did seem to like children, but preferably at a professional distance. Both wore tailored clothing, Dr. Baker's more so than Ida Wylie's. Jo Baker explained that she "badly needed protective coloring" when she first went to work in the New York Board of Health, and so decided to look as unfeminine as possible. The disguise worked so well that a fellow doctor was once berating women in professions with Dr. Baker, who stopped him and asked, "What kind of a creature do you think you are talking to now?" The other doctor blushed and answered, "Good Lord, I'd entirely forgotten that you were a woman."[38]

The relationship between Jo and Ida seems to have lasted without too many problems until Dr. Baker's death in 1945. By then, the two women had shared a home with Dr. Louise Pearce first in Princeton, then Belle Mead, New Jersey, for several years. It may be that what was once a couple became a triangle after the move from New York, with Ida Wylie the apex of the emotional threesome. This seems to be a fairly accurate description, from an account of Ida and Jo's trip in 1934 to visit Ida's old friends, novelist Radclyffe Hall and her lover, Lady Una Troubridge. "John" as Radclyffe Hall was called by her friends (and herself) was in the throes of a torrid new love affair while still pledging her undying love to an outwardly calm, inwardly raging Una.

When Ida Wylie lunched on October 19, bringing her elderly American girlfriend Dr. "Joe" Baker, the spectacle threw Una into a fresh depression. Ida's promiscuity was notorious and the misery that Una detected in Joe's face she judged "a living indictment of Ida's thoughtless sexual selfishness." It was the nearest she could bring herself to blame John.[39]

Certainly, after Dr. Jo Baker died, Ida seems to have transferred her affections to Louise, dedicating at least two novels to Pearce. They were known as "special friends" to the faculty of the Women's Medical College in Philadelphia, where Louise was President. Dr. Pearce continued to wear a bracelet given to her by Dr. Baker, with a charm shaped as a map of the state of New Jersey, a jewel embedded where the threesome's mutual home was located.

Besides these two well-known Heterodite couples, Helen Hull and her lifelong partner Mable Louise Robinson (who never joined Heterodoxy) were also known as an established married couple. As noted before, they met as instructors at Wellesley College, established an urban life as authors and college instructors at Columbia University, while spending their summers at their home in Maine. It took the long illness and death of Mable Louise Robinson to sever their relationship.

Lawyer turned theater agent and producer Helen Arthur lived her life in a deeply committed relationship with Agnes Morgan. They shared a love for off-Broadway and experimental "little" theater, often working together as producer and director at the Neighborhood Playhouse and summer theaters in the Northeast. Helen Arthur's tempestuous relationship with social worker and settlement house founder Lillian Wald has been documented by historian Blanche Wiesen Cook in her revealing article, "Female Support Networks and Political Activism."[40]

Anne Herendeen

The lesbians of Heterodoxy were discussed in letters between other club members (although never called "lesbians"), and acknowledged in addressing Christmas cards to the couple. Good wishes were sent to the other partner whenever anyone wrote to her lover. Although more research needs to be done to verify my intuition, bits and pieces of scattered information lead me to add seven other women as probable lesbians: Lou Rogers, Anne Herendeen, Kathleen de Vere Taylor, Frances Maule, Myran Louise Grant, Gertrude Williams and Ellen La Motte.

Problems and questions raised in researching Lou Rogers show some of the issues in uncovering lesbian history. In place of a photograph on her Heterodoxy album page, she placed a copy of her newsletter for listeners to her animal care radio show. Later, on Elizabeth Watson's page, a large pen-and-ink sketch shows a tiny person bundled up in a coat, stovepipe hat, holding a tiny whip in her hand. She is looking up at a giantess in a long dark coat, flowing fur scarf, and an absolutely huge fur muff. Nearly a dozen grinning cats, dogs, and chickens dash in front of the couple, not looking in the least afraid of the tiny person's whip. The inscription reads:

> Hello Marie! It's plain to see
> That friends have not deserted thee
> The joy is writ upon your pliz
> So here comes Lou and here come Liz
> With their glad gimmicks
> Treat them well—and then
> All troubles go to Hell. [41]

In 1978, *These Modern Women* was published, pulling together women's autobiographical essays first published anonymously in *The Nation* in 1926-1927. Several authors were finally identified as Heterodoxy members, including Lou Rogers. In her sketch of her life, she describes a happy, adventurous life, beginning with a very physically active childhood in Maine.

> Father and Mother succeeded in leaving us children a wide freedom of choice. After I left home it never occurred to me to lay any of my decisions before my parents nor did it ever occur to me that their disagreements with my decisions or ways of life could make any real difference in their feeling toward me. [42]

She "plunged into the world," taking art classes after moving to Boston, then "became obsessed with the idea of teaching an elocution and physical culture system" taught at a school in Washington, D.C.

> With a girl I had met in the school I decided . . . to go West from Chicago and organize physical-culture classes from town to town. We reached Chicago and our last penny at the same moment. My friend was pretty and amiable but quite unwilling to stand the gaff of hard work, so I undertook to support both of us. [43]

A year later, she was back in New York City, apparently sans girlfriend and broke again. Lou Rogers decided to put her drawing talents to use as a political cartoonist, and soon her cartoons began to appear in many of the liberal newspapers. Throughout this narrative of her life,

she never once mentions a male, except as a teacher or prospective employer. Art historian Alice Sheppard has established that Lou Rogers was actually married to a man when she wrote this account, which was published when she was in her fifties. Yet I find the following discussion of her love life very evocative of a woman covering up the fact that at least some of her love affairs have been with women. This would have been a natural response to the rising homophobia of America in the mid-1920s. Lou Rogers wrote:

> Whether in the years since then I have accomplished anything worth while or not, I have throughly enjoyed living. Love is no stranger to me. My love affairs began in childhood and have been going on ever since in varying kinds and with as many results. Love is good wherever it comes from. I am married now, and I find that good, too. Economic freedom is good, and I still have it. But it seems to me that in these days of rapidly increasing fair play between a man and a woman, neither economic dependence or independence makes much difference. It is the spirit of cooperation that counts and enables people to make adjustments both inside and outside of their relationship.[44]

Further research by Alice Sheppard and others on this elusive yet seemingly open, delightful woman may yet uncover information that will clarify what Lou Rogers meant when she said that "Love is good wherever it comes from."

Heterodoxy's lesbian members were a strong presence in the group. One of the most intriguing things to me in researching the organization has been the revelation that most of the hetersexual and lesbian members accepted their differences in sexual/affectional partners and were mutually supportive throughout their lives. Of course, it helped that even the heteroseuxal women were usually in non-traditional relationships, and few would have tolerated a patriarchal, overbearing husband. Heterodites were, on the whole, women-loving and women-centered. Also, those who placed a man/husband at the center of their lives may have believed that the women couples of Heterodoxy were "just good friends." This could have occurred not only because many heterosexuals have sexual blinders on when observing two single women together, but also because the lesbian couples in the club did not fit the sometimes frightening popular stereotypes of deviant, sex-mad women, incapable of handling responsibility or staying out of bed longer than five minutes at a time. (I hope that under those competent exteriors, Heterodite lesbians lived up to at least some parts of that stereotype, some of the time.)

My initial pleased reaction in believing that Heterodoxy avoided a lesbian/straight split reveals more about recent feminist history of the "second wave" of feminism than it does about feminist groups of the early twentieth century. Not having studied more than a couple of those early groups, I have no idea whether any of them recgonized openly the lesbians in their midst. But as personal witness to more than one battle along the sexual barricades within women's organizations of the 1960s and 70s, I clearly recall the tension, mistrust, anger and sometimes open disgust displayed between these two factions. I have learned to regard friendship between a lesbian and a straight woman as a rare, fragile relationship, especially in a group context where differing needs, priorities and goals often break down the communication between the two camps. I am sure that not all of Heterodoxy's members were the best of friends outside the club. Still, many went out of their way in times of trouble to offer their support across political and sexual lines. A small example was Helen Arthur's warm note of sympathy to Fola La Follette when Fola's mother died:

> I can't tell you how stunned and saddened I was when I read the news of your dear Mother's death. . . . one of the finest women of this generation. . . . I want you to know that the one time I saw your mother remains for me a vivid memory of a great and gracious soul.
>
> Agnes and I are here for a little holiday after a hard summer's work at a little theater in Mt. Kino. We go back to our bungalow in Pleasantville next Wednesday. . . . Marie Howe is leaving tomorrow—tonight she is playing bridge. She looks well and seemed gay and happy. . . . My kindest regards to Mr. Middleton—Agnes sends you her sympathy with mine. [45]

Marie Jenney Howe's relationship with Rose Young was at least equal to that with her husband, Fred Howe. She dedicated her book to George Sand to Rose, not to Fred. Mabel Dodge Luhan wrote that

Marie Howe's
loving wit helped her accept the sterility of her domestic life. She
was married to a man who was deeply engrossed in humanitarian
problems, who while he was Commissioner of Immigration, made
Ellis Island bearable for thousands where before his time it had
been purgatorial. He really tried to make it a hospitable and tem-
porary home, while in her own home he was one of those husbands
who seems to be perpetually engrossed in thought and never on
the spot. When he wrote his autobiography and his wife read it, she
exclaimed: "Why Fred, were you never married?" He had neglected to mention this small fact. [46]

Howe went back and added several revealing pages to his autobiography about meeting Marie, which have been quoted earlier in this book.
Hutchins Hapgood thought Howe's autobiographical statements about
his wife were "inspiring,"
full of the most absolute recognition, love and admiration. But I,
who knew Marie well, do not believe that she recognized Howe's
love for her, because of her suffrage and feministic poison, which
had gone so deep in her whole personality.
The inspiring thing, however, about the relations such as existed between Fred and Marie Howe is that, when the man and
woman involved are of a superior character, conflicting temper-
ments, though they may bring about and do bring about great
difficulties and emotional conflicts and frustrations, yet keep the
marriage alive. [47]

Hapgood probably did not know that Fred had completely left out
any reference to Marie in the first draft of his autobiography. Anything
he wrote after that was bound to be suspect. Howe's book was published
in 1925. In 1927, Marie Howe was still feeling enormous pain over her
relationship with Fred. She wrote Fola La Follette:
Fred has cabled me from Paris, so he is that far on his way to
Russia. I hated to have him go, and was sick for three days after he
left. I went to bed, could not sleep, wept, stared at the ceiling and
asked of the hard plaster, "Will no one ever stay with me? No-one,
no-one?" And there wasn't even a raven to croak, "Nevermore."
No one will ever stay with us. That's settled. And I am just as
emotional as when I was thirty, that's evident, too. [48]

In 1929, her book on George Sand came out with the dedication to
Rose Young. By then, Rose's name flitted in and out of Marie's letters to
Fola as often and as casually as Fred's. When Marie Jenney Howe died
in 1934, Heterodoxy turned to Rose for advice on the memorial service,
rather than to Fred Howe.

Heterodoxy women valued their relationships with women at least as
much (and often more) than the relationships they had with men. Two
heterosexual members stated it well in their autobiographies written at
the end of their lives. Inez Haynes Irwin declared, "It seems to me that,
after companionship with Bill, my friendships with women stand out in
the highest and most beautiful relief."[49]

The author Fannie Hurst defended her novels which were described
as "women's novels," stating,
It does so happen that I like women. But women as a whole do not
seem to fancy their sex. . . . I enjoy liking women. I admire the

curve in all of nature's processes. Women have it in the body—and mind. The male is given to plane surfaces. [50]

The shared experiences of Heterodoxy members which were the focus of many meetings helped develop strong rich friendships between highly creative and talented women who may not have met or known each other in any other setting. As Kathleen de Vere Taylor wrote to Marie Howe:

> Many are the fine things that you have done for women, Marie, but to my mind the finest is this: You have helped some of us who were timid and unsure to be ourselves, fully and freely—and in so doing to find happiness and fulfillment. [51]

Over the years, these relationships grew to be among the most important friendships in many members' lives. The little world of Heterodoxy was a warm, secure one, an irreplaceable part of the lives of the members. Inez Haynes Irwin stated it best in her own page of the Heterodoxy album. She toasted Marie and Heterodoxy, "who in the midst of this strange universe and this cold city created a little world for us: . . . in which we could laugh and play, talk and make friends."[52]

WHY WE NEED BIRTH CONTROL!

93

Footnotes to Chapter 5

1. Elinor Byrns, "Heterodoxy to Marie" club album.
2. See Florence Woolston Seabury, "Marriage Customs and Taboos among the Early Heterodites," Appendix A.
3. Hollingworth, p. 71.
4. Ibid., p. 98.
5. Ibid., p. 71.
6. Sochen, p. 15.
7. See Blanche Wiesen Cook, *Crystal Eastman on Women and Revolution* (New York: Oxford University Press, 1978).
8. William L. O'Neill, *Divorce in the Progressive Era* (New Haven, Conn.: Yale University Press, 1967). My warm thanks to Susan Sard for bringing this book to my attention.
9. Seabury, Appendix A.
10. Lasch, p. 61.
11. Irwin, "Adventures," pp. 420-421.
12. *Notable American Women: 1607-1950*, s.v. "Elsie Clews Parsons," by Paul S. Boyer.
13. *Notable American Women: 1607-1950*, s.v. "Stokes, Rose Pastor," by David A. Shannon.
14. Eugene Levy, *James Weldon Johnson: Black Leader, Black Voice* (Chicago: University of Chicago, 1973), p. 150.
15. Grace Johnson, "Heterodoxy to Marie" club album.
16. Levy, p. 346.
17. *The New York Times*, February 26, 1942, 16:7.
18. *Notable American Women, 1607-1950*, s.v. "Gale, Zona," by Walter B. Rideout.
19. Derleth, p. 205.
20. De Mille, pp. 10-11.
21. Ibid., pp. 10-23.
22. Margaret Sanger, *Margaret Sanger: An Autobiography* (New York: W.W. Norton, 1938), p. 108.
23. *Notable American Women: 1607-1950*, s.v. "Dennett, Mary Ware," by Christopher Lasch.
24. Irwin, "Adventures," p. 415.
25. Hapgood, p. 320.
26. Scherman, p. 63.
27. Seabury, Appendix A.
28. Langer, p. 68.
29. Middleton, p. 112.
30. Glaspell, pp. 235-236.
31. Seabury, Appendix A.
32. Banner, p. 117.
33. Irwin, "Adventures," p. 416.
34. Jeannette Rankin transcript, Oral History Project interview, Bancroft Library, University of California. Nancy Cott wrote me about this quote, for which I am very grateful. Jeannette Rankin met Irwin and Anthony around 1910 or 1911 in the suffrage movement.

35. *Notable American Women: 1607-1950*, s.v. "Irwin, Elisabeth Antoinette," by Patricia Albjerg Graham. See also Katharine Anthony's letters in the Ethel Sturges Dummer Papers, Schlesinger Library.
36. Wylie, p. 292.
37. Ibid., pp. 283-284.
38. Baker, p. 66.
39. Michael Baker, *Our Three Selves* (New York: William Morrow, 1985), p. 306.
40. "Female Support Networks and Political Activism: Lillian Wald, Crystal Eastman, Emma Goldman," *Chrysalis 3*, 1977, pp. 43-61.
41. Elizabeth Watson and Lou Rogers, "Heterodoxy to Marie" club album.
42. Lou Rogers, "Lightning Speed Through Life," in *These Modern Women: Autobiographical Essays From the Twenties*, ed. by Elaine Showalter, p. 100.
43. Ibid., p. 104.

Ad for book by Mary Ware Dennett

WITH NEW DIAGRAMS, ADDITIONS AND REVISIONS

The new illustrative diagrams are based upon accurate measurements of normal human beings. Certain revisions in the text have also been made, in order to make it accord with authoritative present-day knowledge.

COPYRIGHT, 1928
By MARY WARE DENNETT

DO YOU WANT TO LEARN the true and COMPLETE story of the ten years prosecution of

MARY WARE DENNETT

DO YOU WANT TO READ THE INSIDE STORY of the devious intrigues and machinations of federal agents and of the fetid motives that animated her opponents? All these are revealed in Mrs. Dennett's book, written while her appeal was pending and rushed to press immediately after her conviction had been reversed

ORDER THIS BOOK AT ONCE FROM YOUR BOOKSELLER OR FROM THE

VANGUARD PRESS

PLEASE USE THE COUPON BELOW

WHO'S OBSCENE?

by MARY WARE DENNETT

This book contains the pamphlet, THE SEX SIDE OF LIFE, for which Mrs. Dennett was convicted.

HERE IS AT ONCE a sensational revelation of the tyranny and injustice of a great government department and also a critical survey of the entire censorship situation

44. Ibid. I look forward to more of Alice Sheppard's research on Lou Rogers art, cartoons and certainly, on her life. Her paper, "Women's Political Cartoons: The Suffrage Years," (presented at the Popular Culture Association and American Culture Association, Toronto, March 1984) is an excellent introduction to the work of Lou Rogers and sister cartoonist, Nina Evans Allender.
45. Helen Arthur to Fola La Follette, August 30, 1931, La Follette Family Papers.
46. Luhan, pp. 143-144.
47. Hapgood, pp. 333-334.
48. Marie Jenney Howe to Fola La Follette, date unknown (1927?), La Follette Family Papers.
49. Irwin, p. 413.
50. Fannie Hurst, *Anatomy of Me* (London: Jonathan Cape, 1959), p. 354.
51. Kathleen de Vere Taylor, Heterodoxy to Marie" club album.
52. Inez Haynes Irwin, "Heterodoxy to Marie" club album.

Ida Wylie

Heterodoxy's Last Years

I have already been half an hour trying to think up something both witty and graceful with which to make our Heterodoxy descendants realize what they have missed. But alas, nothing comes except my affectionate good wishes....[1]

In 1920, when Ida Wylie wrote her inscription in the club album, Heterodoxy had survived together long enough to believe it might well go on forever. Yet it did not last the lifetime of all of its members. The date of the last meeting is still unknown, or how the decision was made to disband. Elizabeth Gurley Flynn stated that the club "remained in existence until the late 30s, when its ranks were perceptibly thinned by the death of many of the older members."[2] Dr. Sara Josephine Baker stated that members were still meeting when she wrote her autobiography, published in 1939. The most reliable source on Heterodoxy history, Inez Haynes Irwin, placed the club's demise during the early years of World War II. That would mean a life-span for Heterodoxy of about thirty years from 1912 to 1942 or 1943. However, Irwin stated in her unpublished autobiography that it "lasted thirty-eight years," making the last meeting in 1950. That seems an obvious typographic error or miscalculation, since no source places the club's existence past the early 1940s. Inez Irwin wrote of the final years:

> At first our meeting-place was always in Greenwich Village, but in later years we met in the Town Hall Club possibly beginning in the 1920s, when Greenwich Village had become a garish sight-seeing spot for tourists and a haven for prohibition speakeasies. Heterodoxy . . . lasted until, in the Second World War, prices of food and meeting places became prohibitive. At the insistent demands of the members, Marie remained its perpetual chairman, until . . . her health compelled her to retire.[3]

Stella Commins Ballantine wrote a long, warm and newsy letter on January 13, 1940 to Netha Roe, filling her in on the Ballantine family news, her new status as grandmother, and about the dispute she had after her aunt Emma Goldman's death with "a committee of Emma's comrades" on whether to obey Emma's wish to be cremated. Stella reminisced about "that night at Heterodoxy . . . Emma was in such great form, and how beautiful Marie was that night. I am so grateful she fell asleep in her beauty and didn't have Emma's ghastly end." She went on to describe a more recent Heterodoxy meeting to Netha, who was in Los Angeles.

> I attended Heterodoxy last week and it too was an inspiring evening. First Ida Wylie spoke about the heroic "little people" of England, then we had an Englishwoman, invalided here after a bomb; a newspaperwoman, who had served as an air-raid warden. . . . Her name is Madeleine Plowman. Frances Maule presided, and her (Mrs. P.'s) courage and humor was an inspiration to us all. She

97

was elected unanimously by acclaim. Frances announced the sad news that Maida Darnton died in San Francisco, Dec. 12th.[4]

Many of the founding members were dead or in failing health by the 1940s, and few new members seem to have joined the club after the 1930s. The meager evidence isn't clear about whether the group chose not to admit many new members, or whether membership no longer appealed to younger women. Madeleine Plowman, a middle-aged friend of Ida Wylie's, was probably the last new member admitted to the club before the war brought the meetings to a close.

In late March, 1940, Mary Ware Dennett wrote Netha Roe the last description of Heterodoxy meetings yet found.

Heterodoxy? Well, it has gone along this year with a revolving system of chairmanship—a different one at each meeting—and meetings once a month. It had worked very well, not that all of the old atmosphere is evident all the time, but on the whole it has been fine, a pleasure that is unique, and for which there is no substitute I know of. We have missed you heaps![5]

Netha Roe

The aging members who still lived in New York City and actively participated in Heterodoxy functions found themselves more and more attending memorial services for deceased Heterodites, which had to be depressing. Daisy Haynes Thompson wrote to Netha Roe on February 28, 1960:

> We have scant news of New York friends: the old reaper seems to be mowing them down fast. News only of Virginia Hyde and Mary Parton. For years Virginia has been an invalid (I am always appalled at what the old body can take), but her mind is resilliant, she reads all the new worth while books and keeps abreast of what's happening in this dreary world.
>
> Mary Parton lives with her daughter, Margaret, and grandson, in Wallingford, Conn. Margaret is one of the editors of the Ladies Home Journal and is constantly sent off on brilliant assignments. That means that Mary has the care of young Lem, a live wire. Her life is empty and sad compared with what it has been. Then too, Mary is a pessimist, but it does not prevent her letters from being rare and brilliant documents. She, too, finds life empty with so many of her beloved friends gone before her. [6]

Sad as it was to watch their friends die one by one, the Heterodites often found it even more difficult to accept the physical limitations that ill health and decreasing mobility placed upon them. Members who had been physically active in an era that discouraged women from sports participation fared better than the women whose sedentary occupations and leisure preferences left them unable to put up a good fight when illness struck. Active women like Ida Wylie bewailed their aging fate in a youth, worshipping American society. She noted that in England, people over fifty:

> . . . don't think much about age. They don't limit themselves by it. All my generation are still playing tennis when they have time. Having lived in America, I've had to give it up, because it is taken for granted that a woman in her fifties has given it up. And I realize that my passion for dancing amounts, among my American friends, to a rather deplorable kittenishness. In England, it would be accepted that if I felt like dancing, I should dance. I think this isn't so unimportant as it seems. [7]

Myran Louise Grant would have agreed with Wylie's lament. Grant's wish was that Heterodoxy women would enjoy "elderly winters of rashness, recklessness, and a certain splendor of generosity." She hoped to grow old "full of noble illusions always longing for fresh adventure."[8]

For many Heterodites, that wish was fulfilled. The writers still published new books every year or so; the actresses were forced to change from leading lady parts to character roles but kept on acting; and the professional women retired from their original posts, yet most still lectured and taught their specialties to new generations of women. As Netha Roe wrote Fola La Follette's husband, George Middleton, on his eightieth birthday in 1960, "From my viewpoint, 80 is not epilogue but prologue to something wonderful and best-of-all ahead."[9] Many members continued to be greatly concerned with the political and moral ferment of the 1930s and 1940s. It became harder each passing year for

Myran Louise Grant

Heterodite women to hold on to the optimism of their youth and believe in the political impact of the individual when the whole world around them was in such chaos. In one of her last and most poignant letters, Marie Jenney Howe wrote to her beloved younger friend Fola La Follette in 1933:

> Aren't we living in a topsy-turvy world—a cockeyed world if there ever was one! And yet it's kind of interesting to hang on to life, and to look on at the droll behavior of the atoms that we are.
>
> Hitler and his intolerance! . . . Mussolini and his arrogance! . . . Roosevelt and his swift success, yet what dangers are ahead of him! He must feel that he is standing on the edge of a volcano. . . .
>
> Fred has been in Washington. I am glad I can stay at home. I would rather read about all those upheavals than take part in them. Read about the big events and be content with small things. That's pleasant. The morning paper—murder, crime & war—then I go out and feed my squirrels and look at the swollen river pouring down from the dam. The trees are just the same, no matter what happens. There they have been before we were born, there they will be after we are dead. And if we cut them up, they say nothing.[10]

By March 1933, Marie Howe was in constant pain and feeling "mentally dull," and full of personal despair. She had stopped attending Heterodoxy meetings except on rare occasions. When she looked back on her life, she felt that she had accomplished little that was of lasting value. Her friend Lincoln Steffens admonished her that she had accomplished a great deal: "Neither my life nor yours is going to be a failure.

What we have consciously sought will have eluded us, but what we will have done will be victories, to our surprise."[11]

Earlier, he had reminded her, "You have so many takers of love. Lots of people love you, Marie Howe; I would like to have you know it. . . . I wish you could feel the warmth of our affection for you."[12]

Long known for her informative letters, Marie Howe spent much of her last year keeping in touch with the scattered members of Heterodoxy. In her last letter to Fola, written three months before her death, Marie Howe wrote of Heterodoxy women, old age, and death.

> Rose [Young] had decided to come out for a month, as the noise in NY makes sleep impossible and she is quite worn out. I see quite a little of Florence Seabury. Doris Stevens is in Uraguay for six weeks at the Pan American Convention.

> Paula Jakobi spent last summer at Sconset [Marie Howe's home] after the death of Ann Van Vechten. She is all broken up and can't adjust to loneliness and old age. They lived together 14 years. It is not generally known, but I will tell you, that Ann committed suicide by throwing herself out of the window. She had cancer and might have lived several months longer. This is what is so hard on Paula. The shock was too much for her. It was in Frankfort at the hospital. Rose Pastor Stokes had the room next to Ann's and died shortly afterwards. [Myran] Louise Grant is dying of the same disease. At Heterodoxy we had obituary speeches for Ann, Rose Stokes, and Ann Shinn. Mary Heaton Vorse had returned from a long stay in Russia and, like the rest of us, looks 100 years old.

> Signe Toksvig has just published a fascinating biography of Hans Christian Andersen.

> I shall be 63 this month. Have neuritis and rheumatism, . . .a game knee and other signs of senility. But still enjoy being alive and am ready to go, or glad to stay, as the case may be. . . . I still love you devotedly and miss you and look forward eagerly to seeing you again.[13]

Marie Jenney Howe died of heart disease in her sleep on February 28, 1934. Heterodoxy's surviving members immediately began organizing a memorial service for her. Inez Haynes Irwin chaired the twenty-four member committee, while Netha Roe, Rose Young and Stella Ballantine were the main organizers of what became the most public and elaborate of Heterodoxy's memorials. On March 9, Netha Roe wrote Fola of the details, asking her to send a message to be read at the service if she could not attend. Several times in her letter, Netha emphasized that Heterodites were far more concerned over Rose Young's deep grief than they were for Fred Howe's. Consider the following:

> My personal feeling, as I am sure Inez's, is that whatever Rose desires is my desire, or I mean is right . . . these speakers were mostly first suggested by Rose, after having talked it over with Fred. Rose suggested, and everyone agreed. . . .

> Of course it is desired that Rose shall speak. I know how she would like to, but she says it is utterly impossible, and she will not be urged. I am glad that Rose has the actual work of helping close the house and is now being able to interest herself in arranging the

CARL A. RUDISILL LIBRARY
LENOIR-RHYNE COLLEGE

program for this memorial. She looked so actually much better yesterday. . . . Must turn in—even though I leave so much, so much years of much—unsaid.[14]

Charlotte Perkins Gilman

On March 25, 1934, one month after Marie Jenney Howe's death, the memorial was held in the home of Alice Duer Miller. The speakers included Ruth Hale, Vira Whitehouse, Floyd Dell, Senator Robert La Follette, Jr., David Seabury, James Weldon Johnson, and Carrie Chapman Catt, as well as several others. *The New York Times* reported that Charlotte Perkins Gilman, Harriott Stanton Blatch, Mary Ware Dennett and many other women paid tribute to Marie's services to women and their great love for her.[15] Fola La Follette hadn't been able to get back to New York in time to attend. That night, Anne Herendeen wrote Fola that the service was

> . . . very lovely and the loveliest moments were George [Middleton, Fola's husband] reading your message. . . . Later, it came to me that you should write Marie's biography and call it "Our Woman." Not meaning to place her (which she would object to) among the specialized Great. It would be very much something else. Something unique—the portrait of a Woman who did not choose to be important.
>
> After a year's illness I'm better & doing some collaborations with Caroline Pratt and loving it. And her. And you.[16]

Marie Jenney Howe had founded an organization that gave a sense of community and kinship to a diverse group of women over a lengthy period of their very active lives. Without her nuturing and spirited vision, Heterodoxy may not have been more than a short-lived women's discussion group. But, as the members themselves pointed out in their charming "preface" to the 1920 gift album to Marie, Heterodoxy was surely much more than that. To "Dear Marie," they wrote:

No doubt you sometimes think of us as a little band of willful women, the most unruly and individualistic females you ever fell among. At such time, perhaps you sympathize with that rash creator, Frankenstein, who would fain unscramble the creature but could not. Probably you feel, in these regretful moments, that this hydraheaded Heterodoxy, with its everlasting eating and smoking, its imperviousness to discipline and its strange incapacity for boredom, is something no prudent woman would ever put her hand to. At such moments you are even capable of a dire and terrible threat—you will not call Heterodoxy this year! But it is not in you, woman, to carry out this threat.

For beneath our obstreperous body you know our soul to be profoundly amenable. The real Heterodoxy is a warm and friendly and staunch spirit, in which our conglomerate personalities all have a share, while yours alone is the spell which always avails to evoke and sustain it. It is easier to experience than to analyze, and perhaps no better definition can be given than the words of Antigone: "It is the aim of women not to hate, but to love one another." To realize the spirit of these words is one of the emotional treasures of life which all women desire, many of them fear, some of them seek, and a few of them find. We owe it chiefly to you that we may count ourselves among the fortunate finders. Like Lysistrata, Asparia and Sappho, you have "started something" which, though perhaps less historic, is no less real.[17]

"What a Unity this group of free-willed, self-willed women has become," the anonymous writers of the "Preface" proclaimed. The lesson of Heterodoxy may well be that in an America growing increasingly hostile to women who love women, these women from such different political, professional and personal backgrounds could grow so close together. "What a seamless shining robe the shuttle of Heterodoxy, moving through the warp and woof of us, has been weaving through these years, the garment of comradeship and loyalty, courage and charity, trust and faith and love."[18] Telling the stories of their childhoods and work lives to each other, arguing passionately about their differences and laughing with relief and delight over their similarities, these women formed bonds that lasted throughout their lives. That is not such a small accomplishment.

"It is the aim of women not to hate, but to love one another." That basic message of the Heterodites became more radical as the pre-Freudian era of Heterodoxy's beginnings evolved into the more cynical and sophisticated 1920s and 30s. Since then, the multitude of society's messages that women should devote their lives and attention solely towards men and male approval has proliferated alarmingly, with only the smallest change within the last fifteen years, thanks to the feminist and lesbian/gay rights movements .

In the 1980s, we are again facing a heavily conservative political atmosphere which batters us daily, attempting to make Americans believe that only biological family relationships really count, female friendships and lesbian love are vile and worthless, and women who "deviate" from the narrowly "correct" path in their political, personal, sexual and professional lives simply don't count in the new scheme of things. In today's politically threatening climate, we need more than ever to study women's groups that were able to enjoy their members' diversity without becoming divided. As a friend noted in looking back on many years of working with lesbian and feminist organizations, "Perhaps our imagination has become stale in relating to each other in groups." Maybe, she said, "We struggle too much and enjoy too little?"

We have so much to struggle for and against. More to the point, we have years of hard work ahead of us. In the meantime, take hope. Marie Jenney Howe and her "little band of willful women, the most unruly and individualistic females you ever fell among" did indeed "start something" which still has relevance for us, their political descendents.

Virginia Kline

Footnotes to Chapter 6

1. I.A.R. Wylie, "Heterodoxy to Marie" club album.
2. Flynn, *Rebel Girl*, p. 280.
3. Irwin, "Adventures," p. 415.
4. Stella Commins Ballantine to Gwyneth (Netha) Roe, January 13, 1940, La Follette Papers, Library of Congress.
5. Mary Ware Dennett to Gwyneth (Netha) Roe, March 28, 1940, La Follette Family Papers, Library of Congress.
6. Daisy Haynes Thompson to Netha Roe, La Follette Family Papers, Library of Congress, Series H (Gilbert E. Roe Papers), Feb. 28, 1960.
7. I.A.R. Wylie, *Flight to England* (New York: Random House, 1943), p. 147.
8. Myran Louise Grant, "Heterodoxy to Marie" club album.
9. Netha Roe to George Middleton, 1960, Library of Congress, George Middleton Papers.
10. Marie Jenney Howe to Fola La Follette, March 22, 1933, La Follette Family Papers, Library of Congress.
11. Ella Winter and Granville Hicks, eds., *The Letters of Lincoln Steffens*, 2 vols. (New York: Harcourt Brace, 1938), 2:796.
12. Ibid., 2:741.
13. Marie Jenney Howe to Fola La Follette, December 13, 1933, La Follette Family Papers, Library of Congress.
14. Gwyneth Roe to Fola La Follette, March 9, 1934, La Follette Family Papers, Library of Congress.
15. "Tributes by Many to Late Mrs. Howe," *The New York Times*, March 26, 1934, p. 17.
16. Anne Herendeen to Fola La Follette, March 25, 1934, La Follette Family Papers, Library of Congress.
17. "Preface," "Heterodoxy to Marie" club album.
18. Ibid.

Magic.

To M. J. H.

There was an effect as of bright spheres,
Emerald, crystal, vermilion,
Being manipulated in midair
By a consummate virtuosity.
It is true
That only a few were actual explosives,
But these were tossed about
Just as fearlessly as the others,
Some had the look of bubbles, fragile, iridescent,
Swaying to individual, significant rhythms,
And a few were entertainingly inflammable,
Coruscating in brilliant flashes
At an adroit touch.
And some were neat, smooth, round cases,
Containing authentic, even celebrated
                                    mechanisms,

Mechanisms that you could hear tick.
Others, sound, firm-fibred,
Offered sturdy and serviceable resistance
To vain influences.
It was all like the whizzing of little planets
Along orbits delicately, dangerously interlacing,
Always without collision or fracture.
And it represented the pastime
Of a conjurer,
A conjurer whose arts were secret
And whose charm was complicated,
But whose wisdom and sanity and wit
You found yourself acclaiming with a grateful
                                    shout
As so many original and living marvels

This wasn't, of course, a Freudian dream.
It was a Heterodoxy luncheon.

by Olivia Torrance

106

Appendix A

Marriage Customs and Taboo
Among the Early Heterodites

[This was a spoof on Heterodoxy members' habits, done in the form of an anthropological or sociological research paper by Florence Guy Woolston [Seabury] in 1919. At the top of the original typed sheets is a notation that it was "reprinted from The Scientific Monthly, *November 1919; copyright, 1919, by the Science Press. However, that was only part of the fun, as there was no such press. The reference to the research-minded Russell Sage Foundation was another inside joke, as it often hired women who belonged to Heterodoxy to compile statistics and write up reports on subjects of little interest to the outside world. All footnotes are part of the original paper.]*

Remains of the early Heterodites, a tribe of women living on the Island of Manhattan in the North Seas, are still to be found by the ardent traveler. Relics of their former civilization are fairly well preserved, although data are difficult to obtain owing to the shape of the Island and the great difficulty of moving in either a North or South direction. It was early in the autumn of 1910 that I began my intensive study of this tribe,[1] although I had had contact with several individuals previously.

I found them frank and friendly, ready to share their folk lore and show me their ceremonial dances.[2] Among some of the tribe was a good deal of reticence about their personal habits and previous experiences, but others had an innate feeling for the value of loquacity to scientific observers.

Dwellings

The early Heterodites are generally housed in caves, piled perpendicularly. A cross section would resemble a honeycomb—(Huinig-camb). Isolated dwellings are almost unknown among them.[3]

Clothing

Some of the Heterodites affect male attire for the upper story and would go further were it not forbidden by law. The *Pitokina* or smock is fairly common. In the evening, many of them appear with very slight robing, following the rule—the higher the function the less the clothing.

Ornament Nose

Nose rings have gone out among the Heterodites, but the ear ring prevails among the more prosperous. The use of cosmetics is regular and as the tribe is approaching middle age, the use of henna on the hair is not infrequent.

Marriage Customs

Marriage customs among the Heterodites are varied. Three types of sex relationships may be observed, practiced by those who call themselves *monotonists, varietists* and *resistants*. Most of the *monotonists* were mated young and by pressure of habit and circumstance have remained mated.[4] The *varietists* have never been ceremonially mated but have preferred a succession of matings. The *resistants* have not mated at all.[5] These classes are not at all arbitrary. Some monotonists have practiced variety secretly. Some varietists would like to become monotonists because the marriage union label is useful in some lines of professional work. Many of the monotonists wear rings to show that they have passed through the ceremonial and are nominally the exclusive possession of some male. The scientific observer, however, should not be led astray by outward totems because I have discovered several instances of ring wearing which are deceptive—rings not having been given by the ceremonial mate. Some of the varietists distinguish themselves by short hair, but again, this is not an infallible sign for one or two varietists wear switches or even transformations.

Fecudity

It is generally thought that the early Heterodites are not fecund because undoubtedly *Neo-Mathusianism* and *Sangerism* is thoroughly familiar to them.[6] Of seventy-five members of the tribe, however, I find that 20 have given birth to children. These 20 have collectively produced 31 children.[7] Thus the average fecundity of the Heterodites is 2.31/37 percent.[8]

Taboo

The tribe of Heterodites is known as a tabooless group. There is the strongest taboo on taboo. Heterodites say that taboo is injurious to free development of the mind and spirit. Members of the tribe suspected of a tendency to taboo are frequently disciplined.[9] By preventing taboo the tribe has been able to preserve considerable unanimity of variety in opinion.

Other data concerning Totems, Ceremonial Gatherings, Education and Sex Ideals of the Early Heterodites will be published in book form by the Russell Sage Foundation in 1920.

Footnotes to "Marriage Customs and Taboo"

[1] I was led to do this by my reading of E.C. Parsons' iconoclastic study of *The Family.*

[2] On one occasion I was able to see a dance, *Katosote D'Un Du Four*— performed by a member of the tribe called Red Rose. The woman was partially clad in her brother's BVD's, with fur tails belonging to her sister and many strings of beads, given by suitors. She danced with wildest abandon, frequently throwing herself upon the floor in ecstasy.

[3] Some of the tribe are housed in the upper stories of stables or garages, but the practice is not frequent owing to the high rental for such accommodations.

⁴Sometimes sheer inertia and the difficulty of un-mating keeps the monotonist as such.

⁵True resistants are rare. As virginity is an asset outside of monotony, many varietists assume an outward resistancy. I recall one resistant who had cleverly concealed 18 varieties of mating, because as she confessed her economic status depended upon her virginity.

⁶Two members of the tribe are known to be teachers professionally of this line and a number are volunteers.

⁷This does not include natural disasters such as miscarriages or abortions.

⁸It is not unlikely that this number will be increased during the year.

⁹A favorite method of discipline is to avoid sending them notices of anarchistic, Bolshevikistic or pacifistic meetings and to prevent their obtaining platform seats for revolutionary gatherings. One member of the tribe who has once or twice shown symptoms of taboo has been made to suffer great mental torture by realizing that she will not be permitted to serve on the Committee of Arrangements in the coming Revolution.

IMPRESSIONS OF OUR PEERLESS LEADER
(FUTURIST SCHOOL)

Lou Rogers' impressions of Marie Jenny Howe

Appendix B
An Anti-Suffrage Monologue
by
Marie Jenny Howe

Please do not think of me as old-fashioned. I pride myself on being a modern up-to-date woman. I believe in all kinds of broad-mindedness, only I do not believe in woman suffrage because to do that would be to deny my sex. Woman suffrage is the reform against nature. Look at these ladies sitting on the platform. Observe their physical inability, their mental disability, their spiritual instability and general debility! Could they walk up to the ballot box, mark a ballot and drop it in? Obviously not. Let us grant for the sake of argument that they could mark a ballot. But could they drop it in? Ah, no. All nature is against it. The laws of man cry out against it. The voice of God cries out against it—and so do I.

Enfranchisement is what makes man man. Disenfranchisement is what makes woman woman. If women were enfranchised every man would be just like every woman and every woman would be just like every man. There would be no difference between them. And don't you think this would rob life of just a little of its poetry and romance?

Man must remain man. Woman must remain woman. If man goes over and tries to be like woman, if woman goes over and tries to be like man, it will become so very confusing and so difficult to explain to our children. Let us take a practical example. If a woman puts on a man's coat and trousers, takes a man's cane and hat and cigar and goes out on the street, what will happen to her? She will be arrested and thrown into jail. Then why not stay at home?

I know you begin to see how strongly I *feel* on this subject, but I have some reasons as well. These reasons are based on logic. Of course I am not logical. I am a creature of impulse, instinct and intuition—and I glory in it. But I know that these reasons are based on logic because I have culled them from the men whom it is my privilege to know.

My first argument against suffrage is that the women would not use it if they had it. You couldn't drive them to the polls. My second argument is, if the women were enfranchised they would neglect their home, desert their families and spend all their time at the polls. You may tell me that the polls are only open once a year. But I know women. They are creatures of habit. If you let them go the polls once a year, they will hang around the polls all the rest of the time.

I have arranged these arguments in couplets. They go together in such a way that if you don't like one you can take the other. This is my second anti-suffrage couplet. If the women were enfranchised they would vote exactly as their husbands do and only double the existing vote. Do you like that argument? If not, take this one. If the women were enfranchised, they would vote against their own husbands, thus creating dissension, family quarrels, and divorce.

My third anti-suffrage couplet is—women are angels. Many men call me an angel and I have a strong instinct which tells me it is true; that is why I am an anti, because "I want to be an angel and with the angels stand." And if you don't like that argument take this one. Women are depraved. They would introduce into politics a vicious element which would ruin our national life.

Fourth anti-suffrage couplet: women cannot understand politics. Therefore there would be no use in giving women political power, because they would not know what to do with it. On the other hand, if the women were enfranchised, they would mount rapidly into power, take all the offices from all the men, and soon we would have women governors of all our states and dozens of women acting as President of the United States.

Fifth anti-suffrage couplet: women cannot band together. They are incapable of organization. No two women can even be friends. Women are cats. On the other hand, if women were enfranchised, we would have all the women banded together on one side and all the men banded together on the other side, and there would be a sex war which might end in bloody revolution.

Just one more of my little couplets: the ballot is greatly over-estimated. It has never done anything for anybody. Lots of men tell me this. And the corresponding argument is—the ballot is what makes man man. It is what gives him all his dignity and all his superiority to women. Therefore if we allow women to share this privilege, how could a woman look up to her own husband? Why, there would be nothing to look up to.

I have talked to many woman suffragists and I find them very unreasonable. I say to them: "Here I am, convince me." I ask for proof. Then they proceed to tell me of Australia and Colorado and other places where women have passed excellent laws to improve the condition of working women and children. But I say, "What of it?" These are facts. I don't care about facts. I ask for proof.

Then they quote the eight million women of the United States who are now supporting themselves, and the twenty-five thousand married women in the City of New York who are self-supporting. But I say again, what of it? These are statistics. I don't believe in statistics. Facts and statistics are things which no truly womanly woman would ever use.

I wish to prove anti-suffrage in a womanly way—that is, by personal example. This is my method of persuasion. Once I saw a woman driving a horse, and the horse ran away with her. Isn't that just like a woman? Once I read in the newspapers about a woman whose house caught on fire, and she threw the children out of the window and carried the pillows downstairs. Does that show political acumen, or does it not? Besides, look at the hats that women wear! And have you known a successful woman governor of a state? Or have you known a really truly successful woman President of the United States? Well, if they could, they would, wouldn't they? Then if they haven't, doesn't that show they couldn't? As for the militant suffragists, they are all

hyenas in petticoats. Now do you want to be a hyena and wear petticoats?

Now, I think I have proved anti-suffrage; and I have done it in a
womanly way—that is, without stooping to the use of a single fact or
argument or a single statistic.

I am the prophet of a new idea. No one has ever thought of it or
heard of it before. I well remember when this great idea first came to
me. It waked me in the middle of the night with a shock that gave me a
headache. This is it: woman's place is in the home. Is it not beautiful as
it is new, new as it is true? Take this idea away with you. You will find it
very helpful in your daily lives. You may not grasp it just at first, but
you will gradually grow into understanding of it.

I know the suffragists reply that all our activities have been taken out
of the home. The baking, the washing, the weaving, the spinning are
all long since taken out of the home. But I say, all the more reason that
something should stay in the home. Let it be woman. Besides, think of
the great modern invention, the telephone. That has been put into the
home. Let women stay at home and answer the telephone.

We antis have so much imagination! Sometimes it seems to us that
we can hear the little babies in the slums crying to us. We can see the
children in the factories and mines reaching out their little hands to us,
and the working women in the sweated industries, the underpaid,
underfed women, reaching out their arms to us—all, all crying as with
one voice, "Save us, save us, from Woman Suffrage." Well may they
make this appeal to us, for who knows what woman suffrage might not
do for such as these. It might even alter the conditions under which
they live.

We antis do not believe that any conditions should be altered. We
want everything to remain just as it is. All is for the best. Whatever is,
is right. If misery is in the world, God has put it there; let it remain. If
this misery presses harder on some woman than others, it is because
they need discipline. Now, I have always been comfortable and well
cared for. But then I never needed discipline. Of course I am only a
weak, ignorant woman. But there is one thing I do understand from the
ground up, and that is the divine intention toward woman. I *know* that
the divine intention toward woman is, let her remain at home.

The great trouble with the suffragists is this: they interfere too much.
They are always interfering. Let me take a practical example.

There is in the City of New York a Nurses' Settlement, where sixty
trained nurses go forth to care for sick babies and give them pure milk.
Last summer only two or three babies died in this slum district around
the Nurses' Settlement, whereas formerly hundreds of babies have
died there every summer. Now what are these women doing? Interfering, interfering with the death rate! And what is their motive in so
doing? They seek notoriety. They want to be noticed. They are trying
to show off. And if sixty women who merely believe in suffrage behave
in this way, what may we expect when all women are enfranchised?

What ought these women to do with their lives? Each one ought to

112

be devoting herself to the comfort of some man. You may say, they are not married. But I answer, let them try a little harder and they might find some kind of a man to devote themselves to. What does the Bible say on this subject? It says, "Seek and ye shall find." Besides, when I look around me at the men, I feel that God never meant us women to be too particular.

Let me speak one word to my sister women who are here today. Women, we don't need to vote in order to get our own way. Don't misunderstand me. Of course I want you to get your own way. That's what we're here for. But do it indirectly. If you want a thing, tease. If that doesn't work, nag. If that doesn't do, cry—crying always brings them around. Get what you want. Pound pillows. Make a scene. Make home a hell on earth, but do it in a womanly way. That is so much more dignified and refined than walking up to a ballot box and dropping in a piece of paper. Can't you see that?

Let us consider for a moment the effect of woman's enfranchisement on man. I think some one ought to consider the men. What makes husbands faithful and loving? The ballot, and the monopoly of that privilege. If women vote, what will become of men? They will all slink off drunk and disorderly. We antis understand men. If women were enfranchised, men would revert to their natural instincts such as regicide, matricide, patricide and race-suicide. Do you believe in race-suicide or do you not? Then, isn't it our duty to refain from a thing that would lure men to destruction?

It comes down to this. Some one must wash the dishes. Now, would you expect man, man made in the image of God, to roll up his sleeves and wash the dishes? Why, it would be blasphemy. I know that I am but a rib and so I wash the dishes. Or I hire another rib to do it for me, which amounts to the same thing.

Let us consider the argument from the standpoint of religion. The Bible says, "Let the women keep silent in the churches." Paul says, "Let them keep their hats on for fear of the angels." My minister says, "Wives, obey your husbands." And my husband says that woman suffrage would rob the rose of its fragrance and the peach of its bloom. I think that is so sweet.

Besides, did George Washington ever say, "Votes for women?" No. Did the Emperor Kaiser Wilhelm ever say, "Votes for women?" No. Did Elijah, Elisha, Micah, Hezekiah, Obadiah and Jeremiah ever say, "Votes for women?" No. Then that settles it.

I don't want to be misunderstood in my reference to woman's inability to vote. Of course she could get herself to the polls and lift a piece of paper. I don't doubt that. What I refer to is the pressure on the brain, the effect of this mental strain on woman's delicate nervous organization and on her highly wrought sensitive nature. Have you ever pictured to yourself Election Day with women voting? Can you imagine how women, having undergone this terrible ordeal, with their delicate systems all upset, will come out of the voting booths and be led away by policemen, and put into ambulances, while they are fainting and weep-

113

ing, half laughing, half crying, and having fits upon the public highway? Don't you think that if a woman is going to have a fit, it is far better for her to have it in the privacy of her own home?

And how shall I picture to you the terrors of the day after election? Divorce and death will rage unchecked, crime and contagious disease will stalk unbridled throughout the land. Oh, friends, on this subject I feel—I feel, so strongly that I cannot think!

(from New York Tribune)

April. 11. 1915

SOME WELL KNOWN WOMEN ORATORS
IN ACTION

DRAWINGS by LOU ROGERS

"MAGGIE" HINCHEY (STRONG ARM SQUAD)

MARIE JENNY HOWE (ONE OFF A FEW YARDS OF SNAPPY LOGIC)

DR ANNA SHAW (PUTTING ONE OVER ON A HECKLER)

MRS NORMAN DE R WHITEHOUSE (WITH FAVORITE PUMP-HANDLE GESTURE)

ELIZABETH GURLEY FLYNN (I-MEAN-YOU GESTURE)

ELIZABETH FREEMAN (CHAMPION SOAP-BOXER)

MRS RAYMOND BROWN (RADIATING ENTHUSIASM)

MELINDA SCOTT PRES. WOMAN'S TRADE UNION LEAGUE

A FOOTNOTE BY THE ARTIST.

NEW YORK CITY has been raising a bumper crop of Grade A women speakers. Women with brains and solid conviction. Women who think about the problems of the day and know how to "get over" what they think whether they shout from a soap box on a windy corner or talk straight into the heart of a Carnegie Hall audience.

From Inex Mi'holland Boissevain, looking like a Greek frieze about to leap from the eaves of the Parthenon, to "Maggie" Hinchey, of the strong arm squad; from Dr. Anna Howard Shaw, with static sparks curling from her finger's tip, to Elizabeth Gurley Flynn, painting the air with a sizzling jet of I. W. W. brimstone—all deserve medals and statuettes in the Hall of Fame.

Appendix C

Biographical Information on Heterodoxy Members

This biographical summary contains the names and information on all Heterodoxy Club members known thus far. Some of these women were faithful attendees from the very beginning in 1912, while others only came to meetings when they happened to be in New York City on a luncheon day.

As you will see, some of the members remain only a name and photograph passed down through the pages of the 1920 "Heterodoxy to Marie" gift album. After more than ten years of fairly diligent research in the historical byways, newspapers, and archives, very little has been uncovered about some of the women's lives, their work, their political views, or their closer relationships with men and women. Not even a letter in a more famous member's manuscript collection has been saved, nor a single newspaper obituary found for their name as it appears in the 1920 album. It is as if they never existed.

For other women, such as Charlotte Perkins Gilman and Elizabeth Gurley Flynn, the books by and about them fill a library shelf. Fortunately, I can no longer say, as I did in the first edition, that too "often the books are out-of-print, torn and dusty with neglect." In the last few years, most of the books by Gilman and Flynn have been reprinted. Other well-known Heterodoxy women writers and their works have also been rediscovered, although never as many as I think deserve it. The neglect of Helen Hull's novels and Alice Duer Miller's often humorous books and stories will probably be corrected in the near future, thanks to a new focus on them by feminist scholars.

But for the largest group of Heterodites, a search of hundreds of biographical and manuscript sources still unfortunately gives us only the most incomplete, fragmentary, and yet tantilizing glimpse of the complexity of these women's lives. Granted, as soon as this book is reprinted, several readers will generously share new information they have discovered in their own research quests about one or more of the members. All of this adds to the growing image of the Heterodoxy Club and individual members which we share. Little details appear in letters between members of the club about this woman or that one, such as Marie Jenney Howe's reference to Doris Stevens in a letter to Fola La Follette in 1933:

> Did you see the terrible thing that happened to Doris Stevens?
> Mrs Belmont *almost* left her $50,000 in her will but jerked it back
> at the last minute in a codicil. Doris has had no salary for years. I
> don't know what she lives on.[1]

Sometimes, printed information in newspapers and other sources was false or misleading [actually, after a while a researcher begins to wonder if that isn't the case more often than not]. If I was lucky, I knew it, or someone more knowledgable than I pointed out the errors to me.

For example, in searching for information on Edwine Behre, I read the *New York Times* obituary for Mrs. Charles Behre which listed Edwine Behre as her surviving *son*. I had a terrible moment there while I wondered whether Heterodoxy had been infiltrated by a male. The *New York Times* reviews of Edwine Behre's classical piano concerts during the 1930s reassured me by their use of the female pronoun. However, when the printed information was all I found on certain members, I reprint it here in hopes that nothing is too far off-base. In the course of this search, I became very grateful for Heterodoxy members with unusual names and for all those who never married men (or if they did, didn't take their names). But the greatest find in the years between the first and second edition happened just as this edition neared publication. Patricia McC. Miller, who has been researching author Helen Hull, met with Hull's nephew who inherited his aunt's personal papers. In searching through the papers still in his possession, she came across the only known Heterodoxy membership list, which lists names and addresses of members, as well as six members who were unknown to me. The carbon copied list is undated, but internal evidence makes it possible to date it as probably around 1920 or 1921. This was a wonderful find, and has led me to add the listed addresses (as well as members' addresses found elsewhere), in hopes that someone will try tracking down tax, rental, or census records for more personal information.

My greatest hope is that you will see this listing as only a beginning step towards fuller knowledge of these witty and intelligent women. Search out their books in libraries and secondhand bookstores; watch for their names as screenwriters and actresses in the late-late show on midnight television. May we all look forward to more feminist scholarship on the long-neglected, rich-textured lives of our foresisters, whether they belonged to Heterodoxy or not.

If you can add to or correct any of the information on the Heterodoxy Club or individual members, or if you are doing research on any aspect of the club, please share your knowledge by writing me c/o L.H.E.F., Inc., P. O. Box 1258, New York, NY 10116. It seems probable that my long love affair with these exciting women will not end with the publication of this second edition. Please include information on your own interests, as well as permission to pass on your name and address so that others researching the same person or area of study can get in touch with you directly.

Alsop, Lucile Davidson

Born Oct. 22, 1891, Fort Worth, Texas. Address listed as 13 Van Dam, New York, N.Y. Died July 27, 1935 in New York City, possibly of cancer.

Anthony, Katharine Susan

Born Nov. 17, 1877, in Roseville, Arkansas. Wellesley College teacher; writer. Socialist, peace and suffragist activist. Lover: Elisabeth Irwin. Address 23 Bank St. Died Nov. 20, 1965 in New York City of a heart attack. Buried at summer home in Gaylordsville, Conn.

Arthur, Helen

Born March 29, 1879, Lancaster, Wisconsin. Lawyer; Theater Producer; Stage Manager, Neighborhood Playhouse. Probable lovers: Lillian Wald; Agnes Morgan. Died Dec. 9, 1939, New York City, of cerebral thrombosis.

Baker, Bertha Kunz

Born 1864?, in Erie, Pennsylvania. Possibly Jewish. Lecturer, author, suffragist. Married to L. B. Baker. Addresses: New Brighton, Staten Island, 552 Riverside Drive, 155 E. 22nd St., and 185 Claremont Ave, NYC. Died Oct. 11, 1943, in New York City.

Baker, Sara Josephine ("Jo")

Born Nov. 15, 1873, in Poughkeepsie, NY. Medical doctor; director, New York City Bureau of Child Hygiene. Lovers: Florence Laighton; Ida A. R. Wylie; possibly (but not probable) Dr. Louise Pearce. Addresses: private practice office, 33 West 96th St., NYC; Princeton, N.J.; Belle Mead, N.J. Died Feb. 22, 1945 in New York City.

Ballantine, Stella Commins

(Sometimes spelled "Comin," "Comen," or "Comyan".) Born March, 1886, in Rochester, N.Y. Jewish. Suffragist; anarchist sympathizer. Husband, Edward (Teddy) Ballantine; two sons. Niece and staunch supporter of Emma Goldman. Addresses: 35 Grove St.; 114 West 61st St., NYC. Death information unknown.

Beatty, Bessie

(Sometimes misspelled "Beattie;" also known as Mrs. William Sauter.) Born Jan. 27, 1886, Los Angeles, Calif. Journalist; writer; screenwriter for MGM Studios; editor, *McCall's*; New York radio commentator. Husband: William Sauter. No children. Address: 132 East 19 St. Died April 6, 1947 in Nyack, N.Y., of a heart attack.

Behre, Edwine

(Sometimes spelled "Edwina".) C.1900, Atlanta, Georgia. Studied classical piano in Europe. Concert pianist; directed piano school in New York City. Lived with Alice Mary Kimball and Alice's husband, Henry Godfrey in 1940 at 11 Charlton St., NYC. Death information unknown.

Brandt, Zelma C.

"New" member from Helen Hull's Heterodoxy list; lived at 226 West 78th St.

Byrns, Elinor

Birth and death information unknown. Attorney, suffragist. Addresses: law practice, 501 Fifth Ave.; home, 165 Broadway.

Carter, Bertha

"New" member from Helen Hull's Heterodoxy list. Birth and death information unknown. Address listed as "c/o Lamson & Co., 9 East 37th".

Chamberlain, Mary L.

Birth and death information unknown. Peace activist; editor, *The Survey*; delegate to Women's Peace Congress, The Hague, 1915; suffragist.[2] Address listed as 41 West 10th St.. NYC; 387 Clinton Ave.,

Brooklyn (same address as Mrs. Frank Cothren).

Chase, Daisy

"New" member from Helen Hull's Heterodoxy list. No address listed, nor any other information available yet.

Cook, Elizabeth Ellsworth

(Sometimes spelled "Cooke".) Born Sept. 4, 1884, in Winona, Minnesota. Stockbroker; Business woman; Suffragist. Vice President of Women's Political Union. Addresses: 160 Waverly Place, 142 West 18th St. Death information unknown.

Cooke, Marjorie Benton

Born Richmond, Indiana, date unknown. Writer; monologist. Address: 102 E. 52nd St., NYC. Died April 1920.

Cothren, Marion B.

Born c.1880, in Brookyln, New York. Public school teacher; lawyer. Legal representative of the New York Branch of the Woman's Peace Party; member, Mayor's Pension Commission of New York, Chair of the Brooklyn Juvenile Courts Association.[3] Suffrage leader, member of the Congressional Union for Woman Suffrage and the Woman Suffrage Party of Brooklyn. Husband, Frank H. Cothren. Addresses: 41 West 10th, 387 Clinton Ave., Brooklyn, N. Y. Death information unknown.

Daggett, Mabel Potter

Born c. 1871, in Syracuse, New York. Journalist; magazine editor; writer. Husband: John D. Daggett. Address listed as 142 East 38th St. Died 1927.

Darnton, Maida Castellun

Birth information unknown. Writer; translator. Address listed as 186 East 72nd St. Died Dec. 12, 1939, in San Francisco.

Dawson, Nell P.

Born c. 1870, in Chicago, Illinois. Literary critic for New York Globe. Husband: Allen Dawson. Address listed as 45 West 12th St. Died April 4, 1923.

deMille, Agnes

Born 1908, New York City. Dancer; chorographer; writer. Credits include *Oklahoma!, Rodeo, and Bridadoon*. Liberal. Husband: Walter Prude; one son. Last surviving Heterodoxy member.

deMille, Anna George

Born c.1879, in San Francisco, California. Lecturer; strong advocate of her father Henry George's single tax theories. Suffragist. Husband: William C. deMille (divorced); two daughters, including Heterodoxy member Agnes deMille. Died March 1947.

Dennett, Mary Ware

Born c.1872, in Boston, Mass. Birth control leader and advocate; lecturer; writer. Suffragist; peace advocate, cofounder (1915) of National Birth Control League; founder (1941) of World Federalists. Husband: Hartley Dennett (divorced); three sons (one died in childhood). Address listed as 350 West 55th St. Died July 25, 1947.

Dorr, Rheta Childe

Born Nov. 2, 1866, in Omaha, Nebraska. Journalist; editor of *The*

Suffragist (1914). Suffragist; Socialist; became Republican in 1916. Split with rest of Heterodoxy over pacifism during World War I. Husband: John Pixley Dorr (separated); one son. Died August 8, 1948.

Dufour, Elsie
Dancer. Address listed as 51 West 12th St.

Eastman, Crystal
Born June 23, 1881, in Marlborough, Mass. Journalist; lawyer; editor, The Masses; social and peace activist. Cofounded Congressional Union of Woman Suffrage (fore-runner of National Woman's Party) and American Union Against Militarism. Husbands: Wallace Benedict, Walter Fuller; two children. Address listed as 138 West 13th St., NYC. Died July 8, 1928.

Ellis, Edith
Could be either Edith Anna Ellis, clubwoman and writer, or Edith Ellis (1876-1960), playwright. Evidence still inconclusive.

Farnham, Matell Howe
Born c. 1884. Author. Husband: Dwight T. Farnham. Died May 2, 1957.

Fels, Mary
Born March 10, 1863, in Germany. Leader and financial sponsor of American Zionist movement to send Jews to Palestine. Husband: Joseph Fels, one son who died in infancy.

Fitzgerald, Eleanor
"New member" from Helen Hull's Heterodoxy list. Address listed as 45 Grove St.

Flynn, Elizabeth Gurley
Born August 7, 1890, in Concord, New Hampshire. Labor organizer with the Industrial Workers of the World (I.W.W.) from 1906 on. Socialist at first, becoming leader of the American Communist Party as well as one of the founders of the American Civil Liberties Union (A.C.L.U.), from which she was expelled as a Communist in 1940. Husband: John A. Jones whom she divorced; one son. Lovers with Carlo Tresca; lived with Dr. Marie Equi for ten years. Address listed as 511 East 134 St. NYC. Died September 5, 1964 in Moscow.

Fuller, Sylvia
Information unknown.

Gale, Zona
Born August 26, 1874, in Portage, Wisconsin. Journalist, author and playwright; awarded Pulitzer Prize in 1927. Member of the National Woman's Party National Council, 1921. Considered herself a socialist. Married William Breese in 1928; adopted two daughters. Address listed as Portage, Wisconsin. Died Dec. 27, 1938.

Gilman, Charlotte Perkins
Born July 3, 1860 in Hartford, Conn. Renowned feminist theorist, lecturer and author; edited *The Forerunner*. Husbands: Charles W. Stetson, whom she divorced; one daughter. Remarried George H. Gilman. Address listed as 625 West 136th St. Died August 17, 1935.

Glaspell, Susan Keating
   Born July 1, 1882, in Davenport, Iowa. Journalist, feminist playwright, suffragist. Cofounder of the Provincetown Playhouse; in 1930 won the Pulitzer Prize for *Alison's House*, a play about Emily Dickinson. Married George Cram Cook, who died in 1924. Married Norman Matson; no children. Address listed as 87 Bedford St. Died July 24, 1948.

Grant, Myran Louise
   Librarian at the Peace Conference at Versailles; lecturer for the New York Board of Education. Address listed 30 Charles St. Death information unknown, although she had cancer, and possibly died in France.

Hale, Beatrice Forbes-Robertson
   Born Sept. 11, 1883 in New York City. Actress from a theatrical family; lecturer. Married Swinburne Hale, three daughters. Address listed as Women's City Club. Died March 16, 1967.

Hale, Mabel
   Birth and death information unknown. Address listed as 129 East 40th St.

Hale, Ruth
   Born 1886 in Rogersville, Tenn. Founder of the Lucy Stone League, advocate of women's rights. Journalist, sports writer, drama critic. Editor of *Equal Rights*. Married Heyward Broun in 1917, divorced him in 1933; one son. Address listed 200 West 56th St.

Herendeen, Anne
   Journalist, poet, founder of *Judy: A Magazine*; editor of *Four Lights*, a 1917 antiwar journal of the Woman's Peace Party.[4] Probably married. Birth and death information unknown.

Hicks, Ami Mali
   Born c. 1870 in Brooklyn, N. Y. Painter, interior decorator, writer. Honorable mention for frieze of Woman's Building at the 1893 Chicago World's Fair. Active in Women's Political Union, Women's Trade Union League, and single tax issues. Addresses: 400 West 23rd St., 141 East 17th. Death information unknown.

Hinkle, Beatrice
   Born c. 1870 in San Francisco. San Francisco City Physician, 1900-05; Jungian psychologist; taught at Cornell Medical College. Democrat. Married Walter M. Hinkle in 1892; he died 1899. She then married Philip G. Eastwick in 1909; a son and daughter. Address listed as 10 Gramercy Park. Death information unknown.

Hollingworth, Leta Stetter
   Born May 25, 1886 near Chadron, Nebraska. Educational psychologist; Columbia University professor; early researcher on the psychology of women and of gifted and "exceptional" children. Married Harry Levi Hollingworth in 1908; no children. Address listed as 417 West 118th St. Died Nov. 27, 1939.

Hopkins, Alison Turnbull
   Born May 20, 1880 in Morristown, N.J. New Jersey state chair of National Women's Party; arrested and jailed for picketing White House

in 1917 for suffrage. Saleslady at time of death. Married John Appleton Haven Hopkins in 1901; divorced him in 1927; three children. Addresses: 10th St.; 38 East 53rd St.; 56 East 56th St. Died March 18, 1951 of a heart attack.[5]

Howe, Marie Jenney

Born Dec. 26, 1871, in Syracuse, N. Y. Unitarian minister; founder of Heterodoxy; author of George Sand biography. Married Frederic C. Howe; no children. Address listed as Harmon-on-Hudson, N.Y. Died Feb. 28, 1934.

Hull, Helen

Born 1888 in Albion, Mich. Wellesley College English instructor; professor of creative writing at Columbia University; prolific novelist and short story writer. Lesbian, with a lifelong relationship with Mabel Louise Robinson. Address listed as 322 West 106th St. Died July 15, 1971.

Hurst, Fannie

Born Oct. 19, 1889, in Hamilton, Ohio. Famed novelist and short story writer; called a "women's writer" and "sob sister" for her deft handling of emotion and daring sexual themes. Reformist; civil rights supporter. President of Author's Guild of America. At one time employed Zora Neale Hurston as her secretary. Married Jacques S. Danielson in 1914; choose to live in separate homes "to meet their individual needs." No children. Address listed as 12 West 69th St. Died 1968.

Hyde, Virginia Douglas

Birth information unknown. Actress; suffragist. National Woman's Party member. Invalid in old age, died after 1960.

Irwin, Elisabeth

Born August 29, 1880, in Brooklyn, N. Y. Progressive educator; psychologist; director of Greenwich Village's experimental "Little Red Schoolhouse" Lesbian, with a long relationship with Katharine Anthony. Adopted several children informally and one legally. Address listed as 23 Bank St. Died Oct. 16, 1942, in New York.

Irwin, Inez Haynes

Born March 2, 1873, in Rio de Janerio, Brazil. Writer; journalist; lecturer. Cofounder of National College Equal Suffrage League. Chaired the Board of Directors of World Center for Women's Archives, 1935-1940. Married Rufus Hamilton Gillmore in 1897; divorced. Remarried in 1916 to Will Irwin. Addresses: W. 11th St., 237 Central Park West. Died 1970.

Jakobi, Paula O.

(Last name sometimes spelled "Jacobi" or "Mrs. Jakobi.") Worked for short time as a guard at Framingham, Mass. Reformatory for Women, in order to study prison conditions. Wrote play, "Chinese Lily." Sentenced to thirty days in infamous Occoquan, Virginia, workhouse-jail in 1917 for picketing the White House for suffrage. Lovers with Anna Elizabeth Snyder Van Vechten for fourteen years. Addresses: 129 E. 10th St., 8 East Eighth St. Death information unknown.

Jenney, Nina B.
Born c. 1900. Probably Marie Jenney Howe's niece. Address listed as 11 East 68th St. Death information unknown.

Johnson, Grace Nail
Born c. 1888 in New York City. Civil rights activist; worked with National Association for the Advancement of Colored People (NAACP). Arts and literary hostess and patron. Active member, Anti-Lynching Crusaders (1920s); member, advisory board of National Association of Colored Graduate Nurses. Married James Weldon Johnson in 1910; no children. Address listed as 2299 Seventh Ave. Died Nov. 1, 1976.

Kelley, Gertrude B.
Born c. 1882. Journalist, known as "Pittsburgh's first sob sister" for her articles as Gertrude Gordon in the *Pittsburgh Press* for nineteen years. Address listed as 507 Madison Ave. Died March, 1955, in New York.

Kenton, Edna
Born 1876 in Springfield, Missouri. Author; suffragist; lecturer; book critic for *The Bookman*; historian. Addresses: 240 West 15th; 92 Charles St. Died 1954.

Kilbourn, Fannie
Born Nov. 28, 1890, in Minneapolis, Minn. Novelist; magazine writer. Married Charles Cathell in 1920; widowed; two children. Death information unknown.

Kimball, Alice Mary
Born Sept. 30, 1876, in Providence, R. I. Social worker; librarian with New York Public Library; labor investigator; suffragist. Taught for many years in Working Girl's Club. Jailed for 15 days in Washington, D. C. District Jail for suffrage protest, 1918. Married Henry Godgrey in 1914; Edwine Behre lived with them in 1940 at 11 Charlton St. Death information unknown.

Kline, Viriginia
Born c. 1882. Actress; short story writer; playwright. Never married. Address listed 104 Loring Ave., Pelham, N.Y. Died March 17, 1951.

Knoblauch, Mary
Born Oct. 12, 1873, in New York City. Magazine writer; suffragist. Active in Women's Political Union and Woman's Suffrage Party. Married Charles Edward Knoblauch in 1906. Death information unknown.

La Follette, Fola
Born Sept. 10, 1882 in Madison, Wisconsin. Actress; labor activist; helped form Actors Equity. Lectured, campaigned for and co-wrote biography of her father, Senator Robert La Follette. Married George Middleton in 1911. Address listed on Helen Hull's Heterodoxy membership list as 20 Rue Jacob, Paris (Natalie Barney's home). Died Feb. 18, 1970, in Arlington, Va.

La Motte, Ellen
Born 1873. Red Cross nurse, specializing in tuberculosis prevention; Superintendent of Baltimore (Maryland) Health Department's tuberculosis division, 1910-1913. Grand Marshall of 1912 Women's Suffrage

Parade, New York City. One of the first American nurses to reach the French battlefields during World War I. Decorated by Japanese Red Cross and the Chinese National government for her health work in those countries during the 1920s. Worked on League of Nation's Opium Committee. Address listed on Helen Hull's membership list as China. Died March 2, 1961 in Washington, D. C.

Lane, Margaret
"New" member named on Helen Hull's list. Address listed as 138 West 23rd St. Further information unavailable thus far.

Lawson, Eleanor
Born Dec. 23, 1875, in Illinois. Actress. Address listed as 15 West 33rd St. Died March 22, 1966, in Pasadena, Calif. of a heart attack.

Leckie, Katherine
Born Kingston, Canada. Journalist for the Hearst papers; editor of *New Idea Woman's Magazine*. Suffragist; Woman's Trade Union League member. Addresses: 129 E. 17th St.; 17 East 38th St. Death information unknown.

Luhan, Mabel Dodge
Born Feb. 16, 1879, in Buffalo, N. Y. Author; art and literary patron; important memoir writer. Passionate relationship with Violet Shillito as teenager. Married four times, three divorces; one son. Address: 23 Fifth Ave. Died Aug. 13, 1962 in Taos, New Mexico.

McBride, Mary Margaret
Born c. 1890 in Monroe Co., Missouri. Columnist; writer; most famous for her daily radio program broadcast nationally. Death information unknown.

Maule, Frances
Born Oct. 24, 1879, in Fairmont, Nebraska. Reporter; advertising copywriter; magazine and radio script writer; lecturer. Socialist. Married Edwin Bjorkman in 1906; divorced 1918. Address listed as 116 Waverly Place. Died June 28, 1966 in Woodstock, N. Y.

Milholland, Inez
Born Aug. 6, 1886, in Brooklyn, N. Y. Lawyer, labor and suffrage activist; lecturer for women's rights. Member of the Congressional Union Advisory Council. Married Eugen Boissevain in 1913; no children. Died Nov. 25, 1916.[6]

Miller, Alice Duer
Born July 28, 1874, on Staten Island, N. Y. Poet; novelist; lecturer on woman suffrage. Her New York Herald Tribune column, "Are Women People?" was heavily read. Member of famed Algonquin Hotel's Round Table of literary wits. Married Henry Wise Miller in 1899; one son. Addresses: 138 East 55th St., 62 East 53rd St. Died August 27, 1942, in New York City, of cancer.

Mumford, Clare
Birth and death information unknown. Founded Query Club in New York in 1920s. Address listed as 1 Lexington Ave.

Parsons, Elsie Clews
Born Nov. 27, 1875, in New York. Taught sociology of family at

Columbia University; anthropologist; author; pacifist; folklorist. President of the American Anthropolical Association. Married Herbert Parsons in 1900; six children. Address listed as 7 East 76th St. Died Dec. 19, 1941.

Parton, Mary Field
Birth and death information unknown. A Quaker who worked at Hull House with Jane Addams. Married to Lemuel Parton; one daughter. Address: Wallingford, Conn.

Pickering, Ruth Pinchot
Birth information unknown. Her "girlish poems shocked the campus (Vassar) out of a year's growth of daisy chains."[7] Journalist and editor of magazine *Arts and Decoration*. Married Amos Pinchot in 1919. Addresses: 27 East 38th St., 1125 Park Avenue. Died 1983.

Plowman, Madeleine
Birth and death information unknown. Englishwoman. Journalist. Probably the last member admitted to Heterodoxy, in 1940.

Pogany, Paula
Birth and death information unknown. Possibly related to or married to Willy Pogany, artist, who lived with Edna St. Vincent Millay in 1923.

Pollock, Anna Marble
Birth and death information unknown. Press agent for the Manhattan Opera House. Bred cats. Married to Channing Pollock, playwright.

Potter, Grace
Wrote for Emma Goldman's anarchist publication, *Mother Earth*; reporter for the *New York World*. Freudian analyst. Address listed as 30 West 54th St.

Proper, Ida Sedgwick
Born Des Moines, Iowa. Artist, suffragist; art editor of *The Woman Voter*. Address listed as Puerto Rico. Death information unknown.

Putnam, Nina Wilcox
Born Nov. 28, 1888 in New Haven, Conn. Millinery worker; writer credited with 3000 articles and over a thousand short stories as well as twenty books. Twelve movies, including *The Mummy* (1932), were based on her writings. Invented a one-piece dress in 1910s (the first bag dress?). Married four times; once widowed, twice divorced; one son. Addresses listed as Madison, Conn.; 245 East 71 St. Died March 8, 1962 in Cuernavaca, Mexico.

Rauh, Ida
Born 1877. One of the founders of the Provincetown Players; actress; law degree (1905) but never practiced. Birth control advocate; socialist; sculptor; poet. Married Max Eastman; divorced; no children. Address listed as 59 Washington Square. Died March 12, 1970.

Reber, Mabel
Born c. 1880. Edna Kenton's sister. Married Neil Reber. Address listed as 137 MacDougal St.[8]

Robinson, Mrs. Boardman
"New" member from Helen Hull's Heterodoxy membership list. Address listed as Croton-on-Hudson.

Rodman, Henrietta
Born 1878 in Astoria, N. Y. Socialist; organized Liberal Club in Greenwich Village, as well as the Feminist Alliance in 1912. Vocational guidance instructor in New York public schools; suffragist. Active in Consumer's League and the Women's Trade Union League. Never married. Addresses: 174 25th St., Elmhurst, Long Island; 315 East 17th St., N.Y. Died 1923.

Roe, Gwyneth King ("Netha")
Born 1868 in Eldora, Iowa. Taught physical culture in South Dakota, Washington, D. C., and Madison, Wis. Eventually owned her own studio in New York City, where several Heterodites exercised. Married Gilbert E. Roe in 1889; several children. Addresses: 498 West End Ave.; 55 Liberty St.; 25 West 43rd St. Died 1968.

Rogers, Lou
Born 1880 in Patten, Maine. Artist; radio broadcaster; radical political cartoonist; suffragist. Married Howard Smith. Address listed as 56 Greenwich Ave. Died in early 1950s.

Rohe, Alice
Born Lawrence, Kansas. Newspaper drama critic and book critic; magazine writer; suffragist. Death information unknown.

Seabury, Florence Guy Woolston
Born April 1881, in Montclair, N. J. Socialist turned Democrat. Fellow at Russell Sage Foundation; suffragist; labor movement and settlement house worker. Editor of the *Woman Voter*; taught psychology. Married Howard B. Woolston; then David Seabury. Addresses: 421 W. 121st St.; 237 East 104th St. Died Oct. 7, 1951 in Ossining, N. Y.

Shaw, Mary
Born Jan. 25, 1854, in Boston. Actress; "ardent feminist." Woman's Peace Party vice-chair. Married twice, first husband unknown; one son. Second marriage to Duc de Brissac in 1885, divorced. Address listed as Hotel Wellington, Seventh Ave. & 55th St. Died May 18, 1929 in New York City of heart disease.

Shinn, Anne O'Hagan
Born Washington, D. C. Journalist on *New York World and Journal*; editor of *Munsen's* magazine; suffragist. Married Francis A. Shinn in 1908. Address listed as 158 Waverly Place. Death information unknown.

Singer, Caroline
Born April 6, 1888, in Colfax, Wash. Writer; journalist; active in Women's International League for Peace and Freedom. Married Cyrus LeRoy Baldridge in 1921. Death information unknown.

Smith, Constance
Born March 5, 1888, in Pontiac, Mich. High school math teacher; Married Talbot T. Smith in 1912; no children.   Death information unknown.

Speyer, Leanora
"New" member named on Helen Hull's Heterodoxy list. No other information available yet.

Splint, Sarah Field

Born c. 1883, in Brooklyn, N. Y. New York public school teacher; editor of *The Women's Magazine*; suffragist. Active in the Women's Political Union. Addresses: 132 E. 19th St.; 142 East 38th St. Death information unknown.

Stevens, Doris

Born c. 1892 in Omaha, Neb. Strong lifelong worker for the suffrage movement. Married Dudley Field Malone in 1921; divorced in 1927. Arrested for picketing White House for suffrage in 1917; sentenced to sixty days in Occoquan workhouse; pardoned by President after three days. Arrested in France in 1928 for attempting to present an equal rights treaty to delegates of the Pact of Paris. Address listed 120 West 11th St. Died March 20, 1963.

Stokes, Rose Pastor

Born July 18, 1879, in Auguston, Russian Poland. Worked from age of four, first sewing bows on shoes, then in a cigar factory after the family immigrated to Cleveland, Ohio. Wrote poetry for Yiddish-language *Jewish Daily News* in New York City; became lecturer for socialism; wrote play titled *The Woman Who Wouldn't* (1916) She left socialism to help form the American Communist Party in 1919. Married James Phelps Stokes in 1905, divorced 1925; no children. Married Issac Romaine (also known as V. J. Jerome) in 1927. Address listed as 88 Grove St. Died June 20, 1933 in Frankfort am Main, Germany, of cancer.

Strunsky, Rose

Daughter of the radical, wonderful Strunsky family in Greenwich Village. Papa Strunsky was a popular Village landlord who was always willing to hear another tale of woe from his artist and writer roomers. Sister Anna married William English Walling, another Socialist millionaire like James Phelps Stokes. Mary Heaton Vorse remembered Rose Strunsky most for "storing dynamite" under her bed in a boarding house, presumedly for anarchist purposes. Married ————— Lorwin; two sons. Address listed as Beloit, Wisconsin.

Sutton, Vida Ravenscroft

Born October 1880 in Oakland, Calif. Actress; suffrage speaker; playwright; author and radio scriptwriter. Organized first educational course for radio at NBC in 1928. Addresses: 519 W. 121 St.; Harmon-on-Hudson. Death information unknown.

Taylor, Kathleen de Vere

Born c. 1873 in New York. At first a music and foreign language tutor, she became a stockbroker in 1914. She eventually managed a branch designed for only women customers. She also spoke frequently for the National Women's Party. Probably a lesbian. Addresses: 114 W. 11th St.; 116 Waverly Place. Died Nov. 4, 1949 in Woodstock, N. Y.

Thompson, Daisy Haynes

Birth and death information unknown. Sister of Inez Haynes Irwin; suffragist. Original member of the 1914 Washington Square Players. Married Paul Thompson. Address listed as Bridgehampton, Long Island, N.Y.

Toksvig, Signe Kristine
  Born c. 1880 in Denmark. When family immigrated to Ithaca, New York in 1906, she became a factory worker. Editor on *The New Republic*; wrote several novels and biographies. Married Francis Hack. Address listed as 229 East 48th St. Died 1984 in Denmark.
Torrance, Olivia
  Born c.1873. On Committees of Women's Peace Union. Addresses: 107 Waverly Place, New York; Oxford, Ohio. Married Ridgely Torrence. Died 1953.
Tucker, Mary Logan
  Born c. 1880 in Carbondale, Ill. Suffrage speaker. Involved in a scandalous divorce case in 1909. National newspapers carried headline stories about her charges of adultery against husband, Lt. Col. William Tucker, an Army paymaster. She and her mother were among the very few women members of the Navy League, which she used as a base to advocate "instruction in small arms" in 1915, and a camp for women to prepare for the First World War, including a course in telegraphy. Death information unknown.
Turner, Maude Sherry
  Birth and death information unknown. Address listed as 453 West 21st St.
Turner, Tabitha
  Birth and death information unknown. Probably daughter of Maude Sherry Turner. "Honorary member" of Heterodoxy.
Updegraff, Florence Maule
  Born c.1884 in Nebraska. Lecturer on women's suffrage; novelist. Her sister, Frances Maule, was also in Heterodoxy. Married to Allan Updegraff; one son. Died 1949 in Dallas, Texas.
Vorse, Mary Heaton
  Born Oct. 9, 1874 in New York, N. Y. Radical artist and writer, reporter, labor journalist. Married Albert White Vorse, 1898. After he died, she married Joseph O'Brien in 1912. Widowed again, she remarried Robert Minor in 1920. Address listed as 24 Charles St. Died June 14, 1966, in Provincetown, Mass.
Watson, Elizabeth
  Birth and death information unknown. Member of New York Women's Trade Union League; chaired its Italian organizing committee. Also testified to the New York Factory Investigating Commmission after the Triangle Shirtwaist Factory fire in 1911.[9] Address listed as 119 Waverly Place.
Westley, Helen
  Born March 28, 1875, in Brooklyn, N. Y. Character actress on stage and in nearly 30 movies, including *Showboat* (1936) and *Rebecca of Sunnybrook Farm* (1938). Helped organize both the Washington Square Players and the New York Theater Guild. Married Jack Westley in 1900; one daughter. Died Dec. 12, 1942 in Franklin Township, N. J.
Whitehouse, Vira Boarman
  Birth and death information unknown. Suffrage leader, active in New York. Married to Norman Whitehouse.

Widdemer, Margaret
Born 1890. Poet and novelist. Married to Robert Haven Schauffler. Died in 1978.
Williams, Gertrude
Birth and death information unknown.
Wycherly, Margaret
Born 1881 in London. Stage and movie actress, including roles in *Sergeant York* (1941), and *Keeper of the Flame* (1943). Married Bayard Veiller, divorced in 1922; one son. Addresses: 11 East 8th St.; 108 W. 15th St. Died June 6, 1956 in New York.
Wylie, Ida Alexa Ross
Born 1885 in Melbourne, Australia. Novelist and writer; very active in English suffrage movement before coming to America in 1920s. Wrote several screenplays, including *Keeper of the Flame* (1943). Lesbian with multiple relationships, including Rachel Barrett in London, Dr. Sara Josephine Baker in New York, and Dr. Louise Pearce. Addresses: Germany; London; New York; Princeton, N. J.; Belle Mead, N.J. Died Nov. 4, 1959 in Princeton of coronary thrombosis.
Young, Rose Emmet
Born 1869 in Lexington, Missouri. Editor, author, journalist, suffrage leader. Director of National American Woman Suffrage Association press bureau in 1917. Editor of *The Woman Citizen*. Possibly lovers with Marie Jenney Howe. Addresses: 226 W. 97th St.; 176 Madison Ave. Died July 6, 1941 in Mt. Kisco, N. Y.

Birth Control Review

Mrs. Poor Patient:—"If you're rich, the law don't count."

Footnotes to Appendix C

1. Marie Jenney Howe to Fola La Follette, March 22, 1933, La Follette Family Papers, Library of Congress.
2. I wish to thank Marijke Mossink in Amsterdam, for the information on Heterodoxy delegates to the Women's Peace Congress in The Hague in 1915. She compared the first edition of this book with "the list of delegates in the *Bericht-Report-Rapport* of that Congress." I have not followed up on this information, but as Marijke suggested, you may wish, to learn more about the Congress through checking Degan's *History of the Women's Peace Party* (1939).
3. My thanks to Marijke Mossink of Amsterdam, The Netherlands, for adding to this information.
4. I appreciate Alden Waitt's generous sharing of additional information on Anne Herendeen, Katharine Anthony and several other Heterodoxy members.
5. I am grateful to Janet Albanesius for correcting and filling much of the information on Alison Turnbull Hopkins.
6. My warm thanks to Barbara Page of Vassar College for additional information about both Inez Milholland and Katherine Leckie.
7. Lawrence Langer, *The Magic Curtain*, p. 69.
8. My warm appreciation to Elaine Sproat of Antioch College for leads to information on Mabel Reber as well as others.
9. My appreciation to Nancy Schrom Dye of the University of Kentucky for sharing information on Elizabeth Watson, which she uncovered during her research on the Women's Trade Union League.

Poster from National Archives

129

Selected Bibliography

Manuscript Collections

Beinecke Library. Manuscript Division. Yale University. New Haven,
 Connecticut.
 James Weldon Johnson Collection
Columbia University. Manuscript Division. New York, New York.
 Helen Rose Hull Papers
 Marion Robinson Papers
Columbia University. Oral History Collection. New York, New York.
 Mary Heaton Vorse, Oral History tapes
Library of Congress. Manuscript Collection. Washington, D.C.
 La Follette Family Papers
 Ellen La Motte Collection on the League of Nation Opium
 Committee
 John Alexander Logan Family Papers
 Cornelia Bryce Pinchot Papers
Museum of Broadcasting. New York, New York.
 Fannie Hurst. "Unhappy Birthday." Radio Broadcast, August 6,
 1946.
 Mary Margaret McBride. "See It Now." Television Broadcast,
 1952.
National Archives and Records Administration. Washington, D.C.
 Record Group 65, Federal Bureau of Investigation, "Investigative
 Case Files of Bureau of Investigation, 1908-1924"
New York Public Library. Manuscripts Division. New York, New York.
 Gwendolyn T. Bens Papers
 Emma Goldman Papers
 Alfred A. Knopf Papers
 National American Woman Suffrage Association Records
 National Woman's Party Records
 Mabel R. Putnam Papers
 United World Federalists, New York State Branch Records Wom-
 en's Peace Union Records
Arthur and Elizabeth Schlesinger Library. Radcliffe College. Cam-
 bridge, Massachusetts.
 Ethel Sturges Dummer Papers
 Charlotte Perkins Gilman Papers
 Inez Haynes Irwin Papers
 Doris Stevens Papers
 Women's Rights Collection

Biographical Research Aids

Adleman, Joseph. *Famous Women.* New York: The Pictorial Review,
 1928.
Authors Today and Yesterday, 1933 edition.
Current Biography, 1940-1971 editions.
Falk, Byron A., Jr., and Falk, Valerie R. *Personal Names Index to The*

New York Times. Succasunna, N.J.: Roxbury Data Interface, 1977-82.

Fink, Gary M., et.al. *Biographical Dictionary of American Labor Leaders.* Westport, Conn.: Greenwood Press, 1974.

Foster, Jeannette H. *Sex Variant Women in Literature.* New York: Vantage Press, 1956.

Great Soviet Encyclopedia: a Translation of the Third Edition. New York: Macmillan, 1973.

Greenberg, Martin H. *The Jewish Lists.* New York: Schocken Books, 1979.

Helvie, Clara Cook. *Unitarian Women Ministers.* Middlebury, Mass: privately printed, 1928.

Hitchings, Catherine F. *Universalist and Unitarian Women Ministers.* New York: Universalist Historical Society, 1975.

Ireland, Norma. *Index to Women of the World.* Westwood, Mass: Faxon, 1970.

Kunitz, Stanley J., ed. *Twentieth Century Authors.* 1955 edition.

Lamporski, Richard. *Whatever Became of . . . ?* New York: Crown Pubs., 1967-74.

Living Authors. 1931 edition.

Mainiero, Lina, ed. *American Women Writers: From the Colonial Times to the Present.* 3 vols. New York: Frederick Ungar, 1979.

Manning, Beverly. *Index to American Women Speakers: 1828-1978.* Metuchen, N.J.: The Scarecrow Press, 1980.

Marshall, Alice Kahler. *Pen Names of Women Writers.* Camp Hill, Penn: privately printed, 1985.

National Cyclopedia of American Biography.

New York Geneological and Biography Record. 1870-1977.

Notable American Women, 1607-1950. 3 volumes.

Notable American Women, 1951-1975. 1 volume.

Overton, Grant M. *Women Who Make Our Novels.* New York: Moffat, Yard & Co., 1918.

Performing Arts Biography Master Index. 2nd edition. 1981.

Perry, Jeb H. *Variety Obits: An Index to Obituaries in Variety, 1905-1978.* Metuchen, N.J. & London: The Scarecrow Press, 1980.

Principal Women of America: Vol. III. 1940 edition.

Rigdon, Walter, ed. *The Biographical Dictionary and Who's Who of the American Theater.* New York: James H. Heineman, Inc., 1966.

Ross, Ishbel. *Ladies of the Press: The Story of Women in Journalism by an Insider.* New York: , 1936.

Rossiter, Margaret W. *Women Scientists in America: Struggles and Strategies to 1940.* Baltimore, Maryland: Johns Hopkins University Press, 1982.

Stoddard, Anne. *Topflight: Famous American Women.* New York: T. Nelson, 1946.

Taves, Isabella. *Successful Women.* New York: Dutton, 1943.

Warfel, Harry R. *American Novelists of Today.* New York: American Book Co., 1951.

Who Was Who in American History: Arts and Letters.
Who Was Who in the Theater, 1912-1976. 4 vols.
Willard, Frances, and Mary A. Livermore, eds. *A Woman of the Century.* Buffalo, N.Y.: C. W. Moulton, 1893.
Women of Today International. 1925 edition.
Women Today. 1933 edition.
Women's Who's Who of America, 1914-1915.

Newspapers
The New York Times, 1912-1971. New York, New York.

Periodicals
The Crisis, 1910-1940.
The Forerunner, 1909-1916.
Greenwich Village, 1915-1916.
Greenwich Village Spectator, 1917-1918.
The Ink Pot, 1916.
Judy, a Magazine, 1919.
The Ladder, 1956-1972.
The Liberator, 1918-1921.
The Masses, 1911-1917.
The Quill, 1917-1926.
The Woman's Journal, 1900-1920.

Selected General Reference Books and Articles
Aaron, Daniel. *Writers on the Left: Episodes in American Literary Communism.* New York: Harcourt, Brace & World, 1961.

Baker, Michael. *Our Three Selves: The Life of Radclyffe Hall.* New York: William Morrow, 1985.

Banner, Lois W. *Women in Modern America: A Brief History.* New York: Harcourt Brace Jovanovich, 1974.

Baum, Charlotte; Hyman, Paula, and Michel, Sonia. *The Jewish Woman in America.* New York: The Dial Press, 1976.

Blair, Karen J. *The Clubwoman as Feminist: True Womanhood Redefined, 1868-1914.* New York: Holmes & Meier, 1980.

Breckinridge, Sophonisiba P. *Women in the Twentieth Century.* New York: McGraw Hill, 1933.

Broun, Heywood Hale. *Whose Little Boy Are You?* New York: St. Martin's Press, 1983.

Bruere, Martha Bensley and Beard, Mary Ritter, eds. *Laughing Their Way: Women's Humor in America.* New York: Macmillan, 1934.

Cavallo, Diana. *The Lower East Side: A Portrait in Time.* With Photos by Leo Stashin. New York: Crowell-Collier Press, 1971.

Churchill, Allen. *The Improper Bohemians: A Re-Creation of Greenwich Village in Its Heyday.* New York: Dutton, 1959.

Cohen, Stanley. "A Study in Nativism: The American Red Scare of 1919-1920." In *Twentieth Century America: Recent Interpretations,* pp. 88-109. Edited by Barton J. Bernstein and Allen J. Matusow. New York: Harcourt, Brace & World, 1969.

Creel, George. *Rebel at Large: Recollections of Fifty Crowded Years.*

New York: G. P. Putnam's Sons, 1947.

Dell, Floyd. *Homecoming*. New York: Farrar & Rinehart, 1933.

——————————. *Love in Grenwich Village*. Freeport, New York: Books for Libraries Press, 1926.

Derleth, August. *Still Small Voice: The Biography of Zona Gale*. New York: D. Appleton Century, 1940.

Dunning, John. *Tune In Yesterday: The Ultimate Enclyclopedia of Old-Time Radio, 1925-1976*. Englewood Cliffs, N.J.: Prentice Hall, Inc., 1976.

Eastman, Max. *Enjoyment of Living*. New York: Harper & Brothers, 1948.

——————————. *Love and Revolution*. New York: Random House, 1964.

Eisenstein, Sarah. *Give Us Bread But Give Us Roses: Working Women's Consciousness in the United States, 1890 to the First World War*. Boston, Mass: Routledge & Kegan, 1983.

Erenberg, Lewis A. *Steppin' Out: New York Nightlife and the Transformation of American Culture, 1890-1930*. Westport, Conn.: Greenwood Press, 1981.

Flexner, Eleanor. *Century of Struggle*. New York: Atheneum, 1974.

Freedman, Estelle B. "The New Woman: Changing Views of Women in the 1920's." *Journal of American History* 61 (September 1974), pp. 372-393.

Freeman, Joseph. *An American Testament*. New York: Farrar & Rinehart, 1936.

Gagey, Edward M. *Revolution in American Drama*. Freeport, NY: Books for Libraries Press, 1971 (originally, 1947).

Gaige, Crosby. *Footlights and Highlights*. New York: E. P. Dutton, 1948.

Gardner, Virginia. *"Friend and Lover:" The Life of Louise Bryant*. New York: Horizon Press, 1982.

Gibbs, Angelica. "Choreographer: Agnes de Mille." *The New Yorker*, September 14, 1946, pp. 32-36.

Goldman, Emma. *Living My Life*. 2 vols. New York: Dover, 1970. (Originally, 1934.)

Goodall, Charles. *The Political Prisoner in America*. New York: Random House, 1973.

Hahn, Emily. *Romantic Rebels: An Informal History of Bohemianism in America*. New York: 1967.

——————————. *Mabel: A Biography of Mabel Dodge Luhan*. Boston: Houghton Mifflin, 1977.

Hapgood, Hutchins. *A Victorian in the Modern World*. New York: Harcourt, 1939.

Hare, Peter H. *A Woman's Quest for Science: Portrait of Anthropologist Elsie Clews Parsons*. New York: Prometheus Books, 1985.

Harper, Winifred. "The Younger Suffragists," *Harper's Weekly*, September 27, 1913, pp. 7-8.

Hilfer, Anthony Charnell. *The Revolt from the Village: 1915-1930*.

Chapel Hill, N.C.: University of North Carolina Press, 1969.

Hill, Mary A. *Charlotte Perkins Gilman: The Making of A Radical Feminist, 1860-1896.* Philadelphia, Penn.: Temple University Press, 1980.

Hollingworth, Harry L. *Leta Stetter Hollingworth: A Biography.* Lincoln, Nebraska: University of Nebraska, 1943.

Howe, Frederic C. *The Confessions of a Reformer.* New York: Scribner, 1925.

——————————. *Privilege and Democracy in America.* New York: 1910.

——————————. *What the Ballot Will Do For Women and For Men.* New York: National American Woman Suffrage Association, 1912.

——————————. "Where are the Pre-War Radicals?—A Rejoinder." *Survey*, March 1926, pp. 33-34, 50-52.

Humphrey, Robert E. *Children of Fantasy: The First Rebels of Greenwich Village.* New York: John Wiley, 1978.

Irwin, Will. *How Red is America?* New York: J. H. Sears & Co., 1927.

——————————. *The Making of a Reporter.* New York: G. P. Putnam's Sons, 1942.

Johnson, James Weldon. *Along The Way.*

——————————. *Black Manhattan.* New York: Atheneum, 1972. (Originally, 1930.)

Johnson, Tom L. *My Story.* Edited by Elizabeth Hauser. New York: B. W. Huebach, 1913.

Katz, Jonathan Ned. *Gay American History: Lesbians and Gay Men in the U.S.A..* New York: Thomas Y. Crowell, 1976.

——————————. *Gay/Lesbian Almanac: A New Documentary.* New York: Harper & Row, 1983.

Kraditor, Aileen S. *The Ideas of the Woman Suffrage Movement: 1890-1920.* Garden City, N.Y.: Doubleday, 1965.

La Follette, Belle Case, and La Follette, Fola. *Robert M. La Follette.* 2 vols. New York: Macmillan, 1953.

Langer, Lawrence. *The Magic Curtain.* New York: E. P. Dutton, 1951.

Lasch, Christopher. *The New Radicalism in America: 1889-1963.* New York: Alfred A. Knopf, 1965.

Lemons, J. Stanley. "Social Feminism in the 1920's: Progressive Women and Industrial Legislation." *Labor History* 14 (Winter 1973):

——————————. *The Woman Citizen: Social Feminism in the 1920's.* Urbana, Ill.: University of Illinois Press, 1973.

Levy, Eugene. *James Weldon Johnson: Black Leader, Black Voice.* Chicago, Ill.: University of Chicago Press, 1973.

Lewis, David Levering. *When Harlem Was in Vogue.* New York: Vintage, 1982.

Link, Arthur S. "What Happened to the Progressive Movement in the 1920's?" In *Twentieth Century America: Recent Interpretations*, pp. 116-133. Edited by Barton J. Bernstein and Allen J. Matusow. New York: Harcourt, Brace & World. 1969.

Marchand, C. Roland. *The American Peace Movement and Social Reform: 1898-1918.* Princeton, N.J.:Princeton University Press, 1972.

Marcus, Jacob Rader. *The American Jewish Woman: A Documentary History.* New York: Ktav Pub., 1981.

Marsh, Margaret. *Anarchist Women, 1870-1920.* Philadelphia, Penn.: Temple University Press, 1981.

May, Henry F. "The Pre-War Rebellion." In *Intellectual History in America,* Vol. II, pp. 132-144. Edited by Cushing Strout. New York: Harper & Row, 1968.

Middleton, George. *These Things are Mine.* New York: Macmillan, 1947.

Miller, Henry Ware. *All Our Lives: Alice Duer Miller.* New York: Coward-McCann, 1945.

Murray, Robert K. *Red Scare: A Study in National Hysteria, 1910-1920.* Minneapolis, Minn.: University of Minnesota Press, 1955.

O'Connor, Richard. *Heywood Broun: A Biography.* New York: G. P. Putnam's Sons, 1975.

Olsen, Tillie. *Silences.* New York: Delta, 1979.

O'Neill, William L. *Divorce in the Progressive Era.* New Haven, Conn.: Yale University Press, 1967.

Ostrander, Gilman M. *American Civilization in the First Machine Age: 1890-1940.* New York: Harper & Row, 1970.

Parry, Albert. *Garrets and Pretenders.* New York: Covici-Friede, Inc., 1933. Revised edition, New York: Dover Press, 1960.

Preston, William, Jr. *Aliens and Dissenters: Federal Suppression of Radicals, 1903-33.* Cambridge, Mass.: Harvard University Press, 1963.

Richardson, Anna Steese. "Is the Women's Club Dying?" *Harper's Magazine,* October 1929, pp. 605-612.

Sard, Susan. "Heterodoxy and the Rise and Fall of the 'New Woman.'" Senior Thesis, Brown University, Winter 1981.

Sarlo, Richard Karoly. *Jig Cook and The Provincetown Players: Theater in Ferment.* Boston: Univ. of Massachusetts Press, 1982.

Sanger, Margaret. *An Autobiography.* New York: W. W. Norton, 1938.

Scherman, Bernadine Kielty. *Girl From Fitchburg.* New York: Random House, 1964.

Schoener, Allen, ed. *Harlem on My Mind: Cultural Capitol of Black America, 1900-1978.* New York: Delta, 1979.

Sheppard, Alice. "Women's Political Cartoons: The Suffrage Years." Paper presented at the Popular Culture Association and American Culture Association, Toronto, March 1984.

Shields, Stephanie A. "Ms. Pilgrim's Progress: The Contribution of Leta Stetter Hollingworth to the Psychology of Women." *American Psychologist 30* (April 1975), pp. 852-857.

Showalter, Elaine. *These Modern Women: Autobiographical Essays From the Twenties.* Old Westbury, N.Y.: Feminist Press, 1978.

Simonson, Harold P. *Zona Gale.* New York: Twayne Pubs., 1962.

Sochen, June. *The New Woman in Greenwich Village: 1910-1920.* New

York: Quadrangle Books, 1972.

Stanton, Elizabeth Cady, et al. *History of Woman Suffrage*. 6 vols. New York: National American Woman Suffrage Association, 1922.

Steffens, Lincoln. *The Autobiography of Lincoln Steffens*. New York: Harcourt, Brace & World, 1931.

Steinson, Barbara J. *American Women's Activism in World War I*. New York: Garland Pub., 1982.

Tax, Meredith. *The Rising of the Women: Feminist Solidarity and Class Conflict, 1880-1917*. New York: Monthly Review Press, 1980.

Villard, Oswald Garrison. *Fighting Years*. New York: Harcourt Brace & Co., 1939.

Ware, Caroline F. *Greenwich Village: 1920-1930*. Boston: Houghton Mifflin, 1935.

Weinstein, James. *The Decline of Socialism in America, 1912-1925*. New York: Vintage, 1967.

Wexler, Alice. *Emma Goldman: An Intimate Life*. New York: Pantheon Books, 1984.

White, Martha E. D. "Women's Clubs and Patriotism." *The Nation*, October 4, 1917, pp. 36-38.

Winter, Alice Ames. "Women's Clubs Today." *North American Review*, November 1921, pp. 636-640.

Winter, Ella, and Hicks, Granville, eds. *The Letters of Lincoln Steffens*. 2 vols. New York: Harcourt Brace & Co., 1938.

Selected Books and Articles by Heterodoxy Members

Anthony, Katharine

Catherine the Great. Garden City, N.Y.: Garden City Pubs., 1925.

"Charleston Portraits." *Yale Review* 16, April 1927, 567-580.

Civilization in the United States—An Inquiry by Thirty Americans. Coedited with Harold E. Stearns. New York: Harcourt, Brace, 1922.

First Lady of the Revolution: The Life of Mercy Otis Warren. Garden City, N.Y.: Doubleday & Co., 1958.

"Living on the Front Porch." *Woman's Home Companion*, September 1926, pp. 32-34.

"Love—Luxury or Necessity?" *Delineator*, November 1924, p. 7.

Margaret Fuller: A Psychological Biography.

"Our Gypsy Journey to Georgia." *Woman's Home Companion*, July 1926, pp. 14-15.

Queen Elizabeth. New York: The Literary Guild, 1929.

Susan B. Anthony: Her Personal History and Her Era. Garden City, N.Y.: Doubleday, 1954.

"Writing Biography," in *The Writer's Book*. Edited by Helen Hull. New York: Harper & Brothers, 1950.

Baker, Sara Josephine

"Facing the Forties." *Ladies' Home Journal*, May 1927, p. 209.

Fighting for Life. New York: The MacMillian Co., 1939. Reprinted w/historical intro., Huntington, N.Y.: Robert E. Krieger Pub., 1980.

"How A Community May Save Its Babies." *Ladies' Home Journal*, April 1924, p. 40.

"Marriage From the Sidelines." *Ladies' Home Journal*, April 1926, p. 37.

Work of the New York City Bureau of Child Hygiene. National Education Association Proceedings and Addresses. 1916: 752-756.

"Why do our Mothers and Babies Die?" *Ladies' Home Journal*, April 1922, p. 32.

Beatty, Bessie

A Political Primer for the New Voter. San Francisco, Calif.: Whitaker and Ray-Wiggin Co., 1914.

The Red Heart of Russia. New York: 1918.

Byrns, Elinor

and Raylett, Helen. *Man and Woman-made Laws of the Suffrage States: a Digest of Legislatives, Good and Bad, For Which Men and Women Must Share Equal Responsibility.* Reprinted from *The New York Evening Post*, Nov. 10, 1913. New York: NAWSA, n.d.

Cooke, Marjorie Benton

Bambi. New York: Doubleday, Page & Co., 1914.

Cinderella Jane. New York: A. L. Burt Co., 1917.

The Clutch of Circumstance. New York: George H. Doran Co., 1918.

The Girl who Lived in the Woods. Chicago: A. C. McClurg, 1910.

The Sturdy Oak. (composite novel with Fannie Hurst, Alice Duer Miller, Mary Heaton Vorse and others). 1917.

The Threshold. New York: Doubleday, Page & Co., 1918.

deMille, Agnes

Dance to the Piper. Boston, Mass.: Little, Brown & Co., 1951.

Reprieve: A Memoir. Garden City, N.Y.: Doubleday, 1981.

Speak to Me, Dance With Me. Boston: Little, Brown, & Co., 1973.

Where the Wings Grow. Garden City, N.Y.: Doubleday, 1978.

Dorr, Rheta Childe

Inside the Russian Revolution. New York: 1917.

"Reclaiming the Wayward Girl." *Hampton's 26*, 1911, pp. 67-78.

A Soldier's Mother in France. New York: ?, 1918.

What Eight Million Women Want. Boston: Small, Maynard, 1912.

A Woman of Fifty. New York: Funk & Wagnalls, 1924.

Eastman, Crystal

Cook, Blanche Wiesen, ed. *Crystal Eastman on Women and Revolution.* New York: Oxford University Press, 1978.

——————————. "Female Support Networks and Political Activism: Lillian Wald, Crystal Eastman, Emma Goldman." *Chrysalis* 3, 1977; pps. 43-61.

Farnham, Matell Howe
Rebellion.
The Tollivers.

Flynn, Elizabeth Gurley
My Life as a Political Prisoner: The Alderson Story. New York: International Pubs., 1963.
The Rebel Girl. New York: International Pub., 1973.

Gale, Zona
Birth. New York: Macmillan Co., 1923.
Mothers to Men. New York: Macmillan, 1912.
Neighborhood Stories. New York: Macmillan, 1914.
When I Was a Little Girl. New York: Macmillan, 1925.

Gilman, Charlotte Perkins
Herland. New York: Pantheon Books, 1979. (Originially, New York: H. Holt & Co., 1914.)
The Home: Its Work and Influence. New York: McClure & Phillips, 1903.
The Living of Charlotte Perkins Gilman: An Autobiography. New York: D. Appleton-Century, 1935.
"Where are The Pre-War Radicals?" *Survey*, February 1, 1926, p. 564.
Women and Economics. Edited by Carl Degler. New York: Harper & Row, 1966. (Originally, Boston: Small, Maynard & Co., 1898.)
The Yellow Wallpaper. New York: Feminist Press, 1973.

Glaspell, Susan
Ambrose Holt and Family. New York: Frederick A. Stokes Co., 1931.
Brook Evans. New York: Frederick A. Stokes Co., 1928.
The Morning is Near Us. New York: Literary Guild, 1939.
Plays. Boston, Mass: Small, Maynard & Co., 1920.
The Road to the Temple. New York: Frederick A. Stokes, 1927.

Hale, Beatrice Forbes-Robertson
What Women Want: An Interpretation of the Feminist Movement. New York: Frederick A. Stokes Co., 1914.

Herendeen, Anne
"Wanda Gag." *Century Magazine*, August 1928, pp. 427-432.

Hicks, Ami Mali
Color in Action. New York: Funk and Wagnalls Co., 1937.
Everyday Art. New York: E. P. Dutton & Co., 1925.

Hollingworth, Leta S.
"The New Woman in the Making." *Current History*, October 1927

Howe, Marie Jenny
An Anti-Suffrage Monologue. New York: National American Woman Suffrage Association, 1913.
George Sand's Intimate Journal. Preface by Aurore Sand. New York: John Day, Inc., 1929; reprinted New York: Haskell House Pubs., 1975.

George Sand: The Search for Love. Garden City, N.Y.: Garden City Pubs., 1927.

Hull, Helen
"The Fire." *Century Magazine,* November 1917, pp. 105-114.
Islanders. New York: Macmillan, 1927.
Labyrinth. New York: Macmillan, 1923.
Landfall. New York: Coward-McCann, Inc., 1953.
"Literary Drug Traffic." *Dial,* Sept. 6, 1919, pp. 190-192.
Quest. New York: Macmillan, 1922.
A Tapping on the Wall. New York: Popular Library, 1960.
"Uncommon People." *Ladies' Home Journal,* Nov. 1935, pp. 14-15.
Wind Rose. New York: Coward-McCann, Inc., 1958.
The Writer's Book. New York: Harper & Brothers, 1950. and Michael Drury, eds. *Writer's Roundtable.* New York: Harper & Brothers, 1959.

Hurst, Fannie
Anatomy of Me. London: Jonathan Cape, 1959.
Appassionata. New York: Alfred A. Knopf, 1926.
Humoresque and Other Stories. Cleveland, Ohio: World Pub. Co., 1946.
Imitation of Life. New York: Harper, 1933.
Lonely Parade. New York: Harper, 1942.
Lummox. New York: P. F. Collier & Son, 1923.

Irwin, Elisabeth
and Marks, Louis A. *Fitting the School to the Child: An Experiment in Public Education.* New York: Macmillan, 1926.
"Measuring the Child's Intelligence." *Delineator,* October 1920, p. 39.
"Personal Education." *New Republic,* Nov. 12, 1924, pp. 7-9.
"We Watch Them Grow." *Survey,* June 1, 1928, pp. 273-276.
"Youngest Intellectuals." *New Republic,* Nov. 10, 1926, pp. 339-341.

Irwin, Inez Haynes
Gillmore, Inez Haynes. *Angel Island.* New York: H. Holt & Co., 1914.
Angels and Amazons: A Hundred Years of American Women. Garden City, N.Y.: Doubleday, Doran, 1933.
Gillmore, Inez Haynes. "Confessions of An Alien." *Harper's Bazaar,* April 1912, pp. 170-173.
A Body Rolled Downstairs. New York: Random House, 1938.
Gillmore, Inez Haynes. "The Life of An Average Woman." *Harper's Bazaar,* June 1912, p. 281.
Many Murders. New York: Random House, 1941.
The Poison Cross Mystery. New York: H. Smith, 1936.
The Story of the Woman's Party. New York: Harcourt, Brace & Co., 1921.
Women Swore Revenge. New York: Random House, 1946.

Kenton, Edna
ed. *The Indians of North America.*
Simon Kenton: His Life and Period, 1755-1836. Garden City, N.Y.: ,
1930.

La Motte, Ellen N.
*The Backwash of War: The Human Wreckage of the Battlefield as
Witnessed by an American Hospital Nurse.* New York: G. P. Put-
nam's Sons, 1916.

Luhan, Mable Dodge
Intimate Memories. 4 vols. New York: Harcourt, Brace & Co., 1933-
1937.

McBride, Mary Margaret
America For Me. New York: Macmillan, 1941.
Here's Martha Deane. Garden City, N.Y.: Garden City Pubs., 1936.
How Dear to My Heart. New York: Macmillan, 1940.
London is a Man's Town (But Women Go There). New York: Coward-
McCann, 1930.
A Long Way From Missouri. New York: G. P. Putnam, 1959.
Out of the Air. Garden City, N.Y.: Doubleday, 1960.
Paris is a Woman's Town. New York: Coward-McCann, 1929.

Maule, Frances
The Blue Book. 1917.
Executive Careers for Women. 1957.
The Road to Anywhere. 1938.
She Strives to Conquer. 1934.
Women at Work. 1939.

Milholland, Inez
"A New Department for Women." *McClure's Magazine,* Feb. 1913

Miller, Alice Duer
Are Women People? New York: Century Co., 1915.
Come Out of the Kitchen. New York: Century Co., 1916.
"Taxi." *Ladies Home Journal,* March 1931, pp. 29, 78.
The White Cliffs. New York: Coward-McCann, Inc., 1940.
!Women Are People! New York: George H. Doran Co., 1917.

Parsons, Elsie Clews
The Aversion to Anomalies. 1915.
The Family. New York: G. P. Putnam, Sons, 1906.
Fear and Conventionality. 1914.
Pueblo Indian Religion. 1939.
Religious Chastity. 1975.
"Sex." In Stearns, H.E., ed., *Civilization in the United States.* pp.
309-318.

Potter, Grace
"The Strange Child Views the Welfare Exhibit." *New York Call,* Feb.
1, 1911, p. 6.

Putnam, Nina Wilcox
Laughing Through. New York: Sears, 1930.

Rauh, Ida
And This Little Life. 1959.

Rogers, Lou
The Rise of The Red Alders: With Many Illustrations by the Author. New York & London: Harper & Brothers, 1928.
Ska-denge (Beaver for Revenge). New York & London: Harper & Brothers, 1929.

Stevens, Doris
Jailed for Freedom. New York: Boni & Liveright, 1920. reprinted, New York: Schocken Books, 1976.

Stokes, Rose Pastor
The Woman Who Wouldn't. New York & London: G.P. Putnam's Sons, 1916.

Toksvig, Signe
Emanuel Swedenborg. New Haven, Conn.: Yale University Press, 1948.
Eve's Doctor. New York: Harcourt, Brace & Co., 1936.
"The Most Unforgettable Character I've Met." *Reader's Digest,* August 1946, pp. 33-36.

Vorse, Mary Heaton
A Footnote to Folly: Reminiscences of Mary Heaton Vorse. New York: Farrar & Rinehart, 1935.
Time and the Town: A Provincetown Chronicle. New York: Dial Press, 1942.

Whitehouse, Vira
A Year as a Government Agent. New York & London: Harper & Brothers, 1920.

Williams, Gertrude
Women and Work. 1945.

Wylie, I.A.R.
Candles for Therese. New York: Random House, 1951.
Claire Serrat. New York: G. P. Putnam's Sons, 1959.
Eight Years in Germany. London: Mills & Boon, Ltd., 1914.
"Englishwoman Visits America in France." *Good Housekeeping,* Nov. 1917, pp. 37-38.
Flight to England. New York: Random House, 1943.
The Germans. Indianapolis, Ind.: Bobbs-Merill, 1911.
My Life With George. New York: Random House, 1940.
Towards Morning.
The Undefeated. New York: Random House, 1957.

Young, Rose Emmett
ed. *Why Wars Must Cease.* New York: Macmillan, 1935.
Henderson, a Novel. Boston: Houghton, Mifflin & Co., 1904.

Index

Putnam, Nina Wilcox 21, 29, 124

Radio broadcasting 62
Rauh, Ida 25, 55, 124
Reber, Mabel 124
Robinson, Mrs Boardman 124
Robinson Mabel Louise, 36, 37, 39, 88
Rodman, Henrietta 17, 27, 32, 34, 35, 39, 56, 87, 125
   Feminist Alliance 2, 14, 57
   New York Board of Education and 67
Roe, Gweneth (Netha) 1, 3, 15, 97, 98, 99, 101, 125
Rogers, Lou 20, 35, 62, 85, 89, 90, 125
   as cartoonist 87
   as radio personality 62
Rohe, Alice 125

Safford, Mary (Rev) 9
Sand, George 59, 61
Sanger , Margaret 19, 81-82
Seabury, David 102
Seabury, Florence Guy Woolston 32, 35, 43, 56, 58, 75, 77, 101, 125
   Marriage Customs 77, 81, 83
Sex
   birth control 82-83
   relationships 75,76
Shaw, Mary 28, 29, 125
Sheppard, Alice 90
Shinn, Ann O'hagan 59, 101, 125
Singer Caroline 18, 125
Single tax 11, 32
Single women 84-85
Smith, Constance 125
Sochen, June 36
Social reform 70

Socialists 32, 34-35, 40-41, 47
Speyer, Leanora 17, 125
Splint, Sarah 56, 62, 125
Steffens, Lincoln 60-61, 100, 101
Stetson, Charles 77
Stetter, Leta
   See Hollingworth, Leta
Stevens, Doris 14, 44, 59, 101, 115, 126
Stock market crash of 1929 65
Stokes, James Phelps 40, 78-79
Stokes, Rose Pastor 1, 23, 35, 40-43, 47, 54, 59, 63, 78-79, 101, 126
Strikers 31-32, 39
Strunsky, Rose 31, 126
Suffrage 14, 25-29, 35, 44-46, 59
   An Anti-Suffrage Monologue 111-114
   Natonal American Woman Suffrage Association 25
   National Woman's Party 39
   Woman Sufferage Party 44
   See also Feminism
Suffragette's march (Photo)
Suffragists, jailing of 26
Sutton, Vida 63, 126

Taboo 43
Taylor, Kathereen De Vere 36, 65, 85, 93, 126
Teachers 13-14, 57-58
Theater, 63-65
   acting as Profession 64
   Neighborhood Playhouse 63, 65
   Washington Square Players 63
Theater Guild 64
Thompson, Daisy Haynes 9, 99,126
Toksvig, Signe 101, 126
Torrance, Olivia 1, 106,127
Tucker, Mary Logan 127
Turner, Maude Sherry 127

HIS HEAD ABOVE THE CLOUDS

photo by Marilyn Humphries

Historian Judith Schwarz is co-coordinator of the Lesbian
Herstory Archives/Lesbian Herstory Educational Foundation.
She was special consulting editor of *Frontiers: A Journal of
Women Studies,* Lesbian History Issue (1978). She lives and
works in New York City.